HEAVENLY HUMOR

for the

Dieter's Soul

HEAVENLY HUMOR

for the

Dieter's Soul

75 Low-Cal
Inspirational Readings

BARBOUR
PUBLISHING

Published by Barbour Publishing, Inc., P.O. Box 719, Uhrichsville, Ohio 44683, www.barbourbooks.com

Our mission is to publish and distribute inspirational products offering exceptional value and biblical encouragement to the masses.

Member of the
Evangelical Christian
Publishers Association

Printed in the United States of America.

CONTENTS

SECTION 4— CALMING THE MILKSHAKES: PEACE IN THE PROCESS

SECTION 5—MIND OVER PLATTER: SELF-DISCIPLINE

SECTION 6—VISIONS OF SUGARPLUMS: PERSPECTIVE

SECTION 10—WORKING OFF THE TOOTSIE ROLLS: EXERCISE

The Fat's out of the Bag: Healthy Eating

The cardiologist's diet:
If it tastes good, spit it out.
UNKNOWN

Those Sweet, or Bitter, Three Little Words

Tina Krause

For there is nothing covered, that shall not be revealed;
neither hid, that shall not be known.

Luke 12:2 kjv

Three little words take on a whole new meaning in middle age and beyond. For those of us past fifty, the exhilarating phrase is voiced in jubilation when we retrieve last year's jeans, button and zip them up, and can honestly say, "They still fit!"

No uncomfortable snugness. No tug-of-war with the zipper. No waistband that curls under a roll of flab or a button that digs into layers of lard. What could be sweeter than that? It's enough to reward oneself with an ice cream bar and a bag of cheese curls.

Unfortunately, on New Year's Day I choked out three other words instead: "They're too tight." The irony of it all is that last year my husband and I went on a weight-loss program. In four months, I lost fourteen pounds of fat and increased muscle, all without thrusting myself into martyrdom while nibbling on scraps of lettuce and dry rice cakes.

So how did I land on the high end of the scale one year later? Blame it on stress, or not enough time to eat properly and exercise, or. . . Truth is, I suffer from a discipline deficit when it comes to food. We all have our weaknesses, and french fries are mine. So is candy, and did I mention homemade cookies? Especially the chewy kind. Yum.

After the holidays, I tried to ignore the fact that my clothes were shrinking again. "I need to remember to adjust the settings on the washer and dryer," I reasoned. Then I went to the doctor for my annual exam. Women hate those checkups, but what I detest most is stepping on the scale *before* the exam. In comparison, everything else is a cakewalk. (There I go thinking in terms of food again.)

So I instructed the nurse not to tell me my weight when—with clenched eyelids—I stepped on the scale. She, however, failed to pass on the instruction to my doctor. "Oh my, you gained twelve pounds since your last visit," the doctor announced as she walked into the room, reading my chart. Now the fat, I mean the cat, was out of the bag and my days of denial were over.

Often, I whisk through life guilty of overindulgence. I appear unscathed until junk food catches up with me, creating chunky fat formations on my body for everyone to see.

Yet all I need to do is confront my shortcomings. The doctor's visit exposed mine, well okay, *one* of mine. Since then I've concentrated less on squeezing into my jeans and more on fitting exercise and proper nutrition into my life. Not only for appearance's sake, but because I'd like to live a long and healthy life to enjoy my family and watch my grandchildren grow up.

After all, "I love you" are the only three words sweeter than "They still fit." Well, maybe there are just three more: "They're too loose."

FOOD FEASTS

TINA KRAUSE

He gives food to every creature. His love endures forever.
PSALM 136:25 NIV

Recently, I decided to board the diet boat to shed some pounds; however, something happened that caused me to jump ship. Scanning a book of little-known facts, I learned that in America, we have food observances for each month of the year. Neither Fourth of July picnics nor Thanksgiving banquets hold a hotdog or turkey leg to the plethora of monthly opportunities to justify munching on munchies.

As I read about these holidays, I gasped in breathless excitement, dropped my calorie counter, and dashed to grab my calendar to fill in the dates. Consider just a few of these food feast days: The New Year begins with a sweet-toothed bang on January 8's English Toffee Day, followed by Peanut Brittle Day on January 26. Besides providing every chocolate lover's celebration of Valentine's Day, February commemorates Solo Diners Eat Out Week (February 1–7), and the month ends with Chili

Day on the last Thursday in February. My personal favorite, however, is Eat What You Want Day on May 11, which gives me guilt-free license to down a vanilla shake with my Oreos. And get this—Turkey Lovers Month is actually in June!

Kids of every age can hoist a Tootsie Roll Pop to the official Lollipop Day on July 20, right on the heels of Gummi Worm Day (July 15). And before the month ends Ice Cream Day, aka Sundae Sunday, arrives every third Sunday of July.

Homemade Bread Day warms us on a cool November 17, and Chocolate Covered Anything Day (December 16) celebrates Ho-Hos, and I don't mean the kind that bellows from the chubby guy with flying reindeer.

I knew Americans loved food—let's face it, commercials flaunt edibles while restaurants occupy most street corners—but I never realized how much. After all, what other country but the good ole USA celebrates food days and weeks each and every month?

Assuredly, some of the sought-after cuisines of other cultures—though foreign to our palates—are meal must-haves also. Consider black pudding, a British and Irish favorite that contains congealed pig blood; or, how about Sweden's lutefisk, a fish soaked in lye?

Mahalet, my adorable Ethiopian granddaughter, loves injera, a fermented spongy flatbread used to scoop up food. And my Hawaiian sister-in-law, Lena, enjoys poi, a boiled and mashed taro root that looks *and tastes*, like paste. Not surprisingly, none of these foods made the food-feast calendar.

James Beard said, "Food is our common ground, a universal experience." God, whose universal providence provides sustenance for every human being and living creature, accommodates us with varying tastes and cuisines. However, too much of a good thing is bad.

So I'm boarding the diet boat again, refusing to celebrate food feasts no matter how enticing. In fact, Peanut Butter Month (March) is merely a few days away. Before then, I hope to sail away from the portly port of too many "holidays." That's a departure date I can't afford to miss. Besides, I marked it on my calendar.

LITTLE CHANGES, BIG RESULTS

MICHELLE MEDLOCK ADAMS

Trust God from the bottom of your heart; don't try to figure
out everything on your own. Listen for God's voice in everything
you do, everywhere you go; he's the one who will keep you on track.
PROVERBS 3:5–6 MSG

Spring break was only two months away, and our entire family began doubling up on cardio workouts and cutting back on calories in hopes of shedding a few more pounds and inches before we donned our bathing suits on the beach. My niece Autumn and I had been doing the same eating program all spring and had both seen great results. But I had sort of hit a plateau while she continued to lose at a steady pace. So, when we were all staying in the same condominium that week in Florida, I watched her like a hawk. I was in search of her secret—what was she doing to lose weight that I had neglected? What was the missing puzzle piece? After a few days of stalking her, I had my answer. While I consumed a few bottles of water daily, I also downed several cans of diet soda, topped off with a touch of regular soda to kill that awful aftertaste, whereas Autumn drank only water. I asked her about it, and she confessed she had given up all soda several weeks earlier. The more research I did about diet soda, the more I discovered how smart Autumn had been to give up that vice. Research shows that diet soda can actually trigger something in you that makes you crave sugar. Also, a 2005 study found a 41 percent increase in obesity risk associated with each serving of diet soda consumed daily. When I read that, I almost passed out. Are you kidding me? I go way back with my love affair of diet soda, consuming so much Tab in college that I stacked the pretty pink cans from floor to ceiling in my dorm room. I knew breaking the diet-soda habit would be difficult for me, and it was. But I have cut way back on my diet soda daily quota and increased my water intake. Now, like Autumn, I am seeing results. Isn't it amazing how small changes can equal big results?

It's the same way in our Christian walk. One small adjustment, one small change can mean big results in our spiritual lives. It might be that God is calling you to get up ten minutes earlier in the morning to pray for your children. It might be that you need to cut back on your time with a friend who is choosing to walk in darkness. It might be that God is asking you to listen to praise and worship music in your car instead of your favorite country music station. Whatever it is, no matter how small it may seem, if God is urging you to do it, just do it! You'll love the results. . .I promise! And it won't leave a bad aftertaste in your mouth or add inches to your hips—woo-hoo!

CHANGING THE WORLD
WITH CHOCOLATE

JO RUSSELL

*Then Jesus came to them and said, "All authority in heaven and on earth
has been given to me. Therefore go and make disciples of all nations,
baptizing them in the name of the Father and of the Son and of the Holy
Spirit, and teaching them to obey everything I have commanded you.
And surely I am with you always, to the very end of the age."*
MATTHEW 28:18–20 NIV

Teaching people in the world around you about eating healthier
is like influencing others to know Jesus. All need to hear, even if
only some listen.

I didn't think my coworkers noticed that, while they chugged
energy drinks the size of pineapples, I drank water. While they tingled
with delight at frosted cupcakes, candy bars, fries, and packaged cookies
left over from the Vietnam War, I ate carrots, fruit, home-baked bread,

and casseroles. When a thief was on the loose in the lounge, many cried pitifully, "Someone stole my soda! Isn't that against the law?" But no one ever tried to steal my lunch.

At the retail warehouse where I work, we rival the Israelite workforce in Egypt, building pyramids. Ours aren't of stone, but cardboard boxes of supplies coming in on trucks nearly every night. While the rest of the town dozes, our team moves pallets and leaps tall buildings with a toilet under each arm. Hours later, we drag ourselves out of the place like overworked stone masons.

Energy is the answer! We all needed it. My heart was in the right place as I thought, *Wouldn't it be a good thing to bring some of my "race cookies"?*

I might as well have said to my coworkers, "Let's all eat a mealworm, grasshopper, and spinach casserole!"

My cookies mimic the ingredients of the popular energy bars but, to me, they taste better. Brown rice, molasses, oats and grains, dates and raisins, and pureed fruit turn into pure energy!

I made the bars, set them out in the employee break room, and waited. Most treats laced with marshmallows and chips disappeared within an hour. Mine lay there like a specimen in a petri dish, growing penicillin. No one touched them as the hours ticked by. Toward the end of the day, one row was gone. No one came back for seconds.

I remembered when, at a local cooking demonstration, Chef Sara quipped, "Cook for your audience! Remember what they like to eat!"

Hmm. That was easy. Chocolate!

I stirred up the second batch of race bars, using chocolate chips, cocoa powder, coconut, pureed bananas, more sugar, and no dates or raisins. An hour after setting them out in the break room, half of the treats were gone. Then, sixty minutes later, there was nothing left but crumbs.

Steering my coworkers toward healthier eating is like reaching out to tell people about Jesus. To some, the news is immediately great! Others need a second helping or more to hear. Some will listen, learn, and believe. Some won't. Keep on telling your story, even if you do it with chocolate!

No Foolin' with a Faux Meatloaf

Jo Russell

*The rabble with them began to crave other food, and again
the Israelites started wailing and said, "If we only had meat to eat!
We remember the fish we ate in Egypt at no cost — also the cucumbers,
melons, leeks, onions and garlic. But now we have lost our appetite;
we never see anything but this manna!"*

NUMBERS 11:4–6 NIV

When a mother goes on a diet, she brings all family members in on the experience whether they like it or not. However, some things we try do not bring applause.

The Israelites had everything they needed in manna, but complained bitterly. They were ready to trade their freedom for slavery just to have fish seasoned with garlic. That can be the same in a family.

I tried vegetarian cooking. A thin, athletic friend suggested it is healthier and less expensive. I started with ordinary things like cheese enchiladas. My teen sons didn't seem to notice there was less or no meat. Then I got braver.

One evening, I placed an especially good-looking meatloaf on the table. It was decorated with so much skill it belonged on the cover of a cooking magazine!

Each of my teen twin sons took a portion the size of a small ham and had a knife and fork ready. The meat cut easily, too easily! It was soft, not firm.

One took a bite. The other tried his.

The look on their faces should have been grateful. This vegetarian food has been around for thousands of years.

Instead, the young men stared at me with looks that would wipe out an army.

I felt like two machine guns were pointed at me.

"What is this?" both demanded at the same time.

"Why, this is a lentil meatloaf!" I announced.

They made faces and rolled their eyes. "We can't eat this!"

Then and there it was obvious my sons were counting the days until they were eighteen, could move out on their own, and eat herds of cows, one real meatloaf and six steaks at a time.

"When are we going to get something decent to eat around here?"

Without another bite, both stomped to their room to use the phone. Surely, someone in this town would have sympathy for them and offer meat!

A short time later, friends picked my sons up for "real food" courtesy of their buddies' mom and dad. I ate by myself, contemplating my flat belly and the lentil loaf. In the months ahead before my sons moved out on their own, I had to find common ground. It couldn't be lentils. Otherwise, I'd never see them again.

I went back to cooking what my sons were used to, so they stayed home for meals. When they moved out, I missed the time we shared. One thing none of us missed was the lentil loaf.

The Israelites wanted to trade their freedom for food they liked. I remember that when my sons and friends visit. How about baked salmon, scallops, or Cajun rice and black beans? God gives us lots of tasty choices!

PICKY-CHOOSEY

DEBORA M. COTY

The wise in heart are called discerning.
PROVERBS 16:21 NIV

For lack of table space, I used the floor of my home office to lay out all the fixings for eight gift baskets. . .flavored tea bags, floral stationery, various writing supplies, and a ceramic fall mug filled with chocolate Kisses, Godiva Gems, Baby Ruths, Nestle Crunches, Butterfingers, Dove dark chocolate-caramel nuggets, and Tootsie Rolls. Imagine how excited the drawing winners at my writing retreat will be when they receive these prizes! I assembled all the goodies into wicker baskets and had just begun to wrap the first with clear cellophane when I noticed the time.

Yikes! I'm late for church! I'll have to finish when I come home. Without another thought, I dropped my scissors and coils of colorful curling ribbon, grabbed my Bible, and rushed out to the car.

When I returned home two hours later, the first hint that something was amiss assaulted me in the form of a crumpled Godiva wrapper peeking out from beneath the couch. *Now where did that come from?*

I was clued in by one glance at my miniature poodle, Fenway, skulking away with a candy bar protruding like a cigar from his mouth. "Fenway! You *bad* dog! Did you get into my gift baskets?" Of course he had. The little choco-dickens. A chip off the old semi-sweet baking block. (Don't worry, he was okay!) The extraordinary thing was that Fenway, who normally employs a dinnertime feeding frenzy not unlike a famished shark, had carefully nosed his way through the smorgasbord of ever-so-sweet options laid conveniently out before him and ferreted out only the best. Just the Godiva and Dove bars were missing.

"You should be so discerning!" my too-friendly thighs whispered to each other as I chased my delinquent dog.

"Teach me good discernment" (Psalm 119:66 NASB). I'm pretty sure the psalmist wasn't talking about chocolate in this passage, but the point is that spiritual discernment—the ability to analyze, understand, and judge from an enlightened perspective what is and is not from God—is important for Christ-followers. Thankfully, the Lord knew how confused we can get when we're so inundated with things *not* from God in the course of our every day, so He sent a Helper, the Holy Spirit, to enable us to distinguish the difference.

Yes, the Holy Spirit reveals the difference between truth and untruth to us, for "the Spirit searches all things, even the deep things of God" (1 Corinthians 2:10 NIV).

In modern vernacular, the Holy Spirit is our spiritual search engine. Our Holy Google. In order to practice spiritual discernment, we must simply engage His willing services to tap into His vast database of truth versus clever lies. Girlfriend, God wants us to be picky-choosy about what we do, whom we hang with, the images we feed our eyes, ears and minds, and even—(shudder)—what we put into our mouths.

With the Holy Spirit as our Helper, good discernment isn't just for four-legged candy lovers!

THE MAN FROM LA MUNCHIES

JANET ROCKEY

Every man who eats and drinks sees good
in all his labor—it is the gift of God.
ECCLESIASTES 3:13 NASB

Obsessed with chivalrous ideals, Don Quixote took up the sword to destroy the wicked and defend the helpless. He traversed Spain in search of adventure. My less obsessive husband roamed grocery store aisles in search of tempting munchies.

I called to let him know I was on my way home from work. "What's for dinner?"

A sudden turn in our finances had sent me back to a nine-to-five job. Tom had taken over the cooking and grocery-shopping chores.

"It's a surprise." His voice oozed satisfaction.

I envisioned roast chicken, acorn squash, steamed asparagus, and salad. This image of nutritional delight included a white cloth on the dining room table, set with fine china, and taper candles in cherub holders.

I walked into the kitchen and found my husband in front of the stove, wearing my kitty apron, stirring something in a skillet. He covered the pan and said with a grin, "No peeking!"

The combined aromas from the stove and microwave quashed my expectation of an elegant dinner.

Tom had set the kitchen table with my everyday Corelle. "Ready in five minutes," he said. "Go change your clothes."

I went into the bedroom and changed into my sweats, giving thanks for whatever he was making. "No matter what it is," I told myself, "I didn't have to cook it."

"It's on the table," he said as I returned to the kitchen. "Tube steaks, baked beans, and fried potatoes." He sat at the table, still wearing the apron. "And there's Moose Tracks in the freezer for dessert." He beamed.

I love tube steaks (Tom's name for hot dogs), baked beans, and fried potatoes. And I could eat my weight in Moose Tracks. But I had hoped for something healthier, especially since my doctor ordered me to reduce my carbs and sugar intake.

I stifled my complaint. After all, Tom had embarked on a new journey in his life. For him to read a recipe from my cookbook would be tantamount to me reading a car repair manual.

Later, I began to drop not-so-subtle hints about healthy eating. He accepted my suggestions with a grimace at first.

In time, ground turkey meatloaf replaced his tube steaks. Tom substituted steamed broccoli for fried potatoes. But sometimes, baked beans are just baked beans.

Now for breakfast he serves oatmeal or cream of wheat topped with a tiny pat of butter and a tablespoon of honey. He makes delicious pancakes, too, drizzled with a scant droplet of sugar-free maple-flavored syrup.

Don Quixote continued his futile search for the wicked and the helpless, never learning from his mishaps. But my Man from La Munchies now traverses grocery store aisles in search of healthy foods and snacks.

Now, if I could only get him to use coupons. . . .

Circumstances changed our roles in life, but God continued to bless Tom's labors.

EYES BIGGER THAN YOUR STOMACH?

TINA KRAUSE

I have learned how to be content with whatever I have. . . .
I have learned the secret of living in every situation, whether
it is with a full stomach or empty, with plenty or little.
For I can do everything through Christ, who gives me strength.
PHILIPPIANS 4:11–13 NLT

When I was sixteen, way back in the horse-and-buggy days, I joined my aunt, uncle, and cousin on a trip to Florida. On the way we stopped at Morrison's Cafeteria to eat. Unaccustomed to eating out (boy, has that changed), stopping at a restaurant was a real treat for me.

I slid my tray past the biggest selection of yummy comestibles I had ever seen: various salad combinations, fried chicken, steaming roast beef and mashed potatoes, hot rolls, and an assortment of pies and cakes.

"Get whatever you'd like," my aunt Alice offered as I, wide-eyed and eager, loaded my tray. By the time we reached the register, I'd accumulated enough food to feed a family of five.

Later, having forced down one more bite, I dropped my fork, clutching my stomach. "I feel sick," I groaned.

With an insightful grin, my aunt said, "Eyes bigger than your stomach, huh?"

Unfortunately, that was only one of many bouts of overindulgence ever since. In fact, if our eyes really are bigger than our stomachs, my eyes would be equal in size to the circumference of the moon.

My tendency to eat more than I need is my biggest diet nemesis. That and chocolate candy. Oh, and chewy cookies. And I love white cake with butter cream frosting, too.

We live in an overindulgent society. Materialistically we want the latest electronics or fashions, while spiritually we want our smorgasbord of prayers answered quickly. Emotionally, we seek happiness void of pain, sorrow, or problems. We desire to grow but shun the growth process. So some of us desire to see it all, know it all, have it all, and we want it all—now. Our "eyes" exceed our needs.

The apostle Paul penned the words that godly contentment is of great gain (see 1 Timothy 6:6), and he didn't mean gain in terms of body fat. God intends for us to enjoy the food He provides without acquiring an obsession for more. Truth is, most of us are only able to digest small increments at one time, anyway. (Or at least that's what I'm told.)

Regardless, overindulgence of any sort leads to big stomach problems, negative results, and eyes the size of saucers at Morrison's Cafeteria. . .or in the smorgasbord of life.

Mother Knows Best

Melanie Stiles

Fools think their own way is right,
but the wise listen to others.
Proverbs 12:15 NLT

My daughter and I are very good at the buddy eating system when it comes to junk food. Since she was the last child living at home, it was soon all too easy to slip into a pattern that included the absence of preparing meals at home. After all, there were only two of us. Why not live off of fast food? The excuses and justifications were far too easy to voice, a situation compounded by the existence of a variety of food at nearly every intersection. Life rolled on and so did our respective weights, until I started to develop a conscience about the pounds we had picked up over the course of several years. As a mother, I started feeling just as responsible for my daughter's pounds as I did my own. I decided to approach the subject gently, praying all the while she would be receptive.

"Honey, we have really gotten thick around the middle. What do you think about dieting together?"

She surprised me with her response.

"Mother, I've been thinking sort of the same thing. We eat like two unattended six-year-olds. But we don't need to diet. We need to change our lifestyle. That's the only way this will work."

Her words contained far more insight than I'd expected.

"I totally agree," I said, "and I've got a perfect 'lifestyle' plan in mind."

She listened quietly while I outlined my version of how we could reverse what we'd done.

"That's not going to work for me, Mama. We don't like to eat the same things, so your food list is not going to match mine. We can agree to stop being counterproductive for one another, but I'm going to have to do this my way."

Everyone knows that a mother knows best, except her own children when they have a differing opinion. I realized arguing with her would be futile. So I quickly decided time would be the proof I needed to teach her a lesson. We weighed in and each got on with our respective weight-loss techniques.

Two weeks later, we simultaneously stepped on the scales. She had lost five pounds to my two. I blamed my lack of loss on the fact that I was older and had slower metabolism. We threw in walking together in the evenings to increase our results. Four weeks later, she was down eight more pounds to my four. At the end of two months, I had to concede that she knew what she was doing far better than I. The tides had turned, and it was time for a daughter to teach her mother new tricks.

I realized God had every intention of both of us succeeding. He was simply waiting for me to grow into the place where I could recognize the truth He had nestled inside the beautiful young person in front of me. And eventually I did.

Everyone knows a mother knows best—especially when she can recognize the voice of wisdom inside her daughter.

TOO GOOD TO BE TRUE

MICHELLE MEDLOCK ADAMS

*"For God loved the world so much that he gave his one and only Son,
so that everyone who believes in him will not perish but have eternal life."*
JOHN 3:16 NLT

I was shopping in a local drugstore the other day, and I passed by a display of boxes labeled THE COOKIE DIET.

Finally, I thought, *a diet I will enjoy!*

I thought possibly this new cookie diet would allow me to eat all of the chocolate chip cookies I wanted in a day and still lose weight. Well, upon further investigation, I learned I would be able to eat only six cookies a day and one small meal, and I had to eat the cookies from this company. Still, six cookies in one day seemed pretty exciting, so I bought the cookie kit! Once inside my car, I quickly unwrapped a cookie and inspected it. Finally, I sank my teeth into it. Um. . .it wasn't exactly a Mrs. Fields chocolate chip cookie, know what I mean? If the cookies had tasted better, I might've been more excited about the diet, but they didn't. So I threw the box of cookies away and chalked it up to another too-good-to-be-true gimmick I had fallen for in the weight-loss/diet world.

Ever been there? Ever heard a radio advertisement touting a program to "lose weight while you sleep" and actually called the 800 number to order it? Yep, me, too. Why do we do such silly things? I'm always so aggravated with myself when I fall for yet another diet scam, and I can hear my mom's voice playing in my head, "Michelle, if it sounds too good to be true, it usually is." When it comes to the world of weight loss and exercise, the old expression that my mom swore by holds true. I have many discarded pills, potions, and cookie diets to prove it!

But, when it comes to Jesus, that old adage doesn't apply. Just hearing that God's precious Son died on a cross for our sins, loves us unconditionally, and has a good plan for each one of us *sounds* too good to be true, but it's not! It is the absolute truth, and I'm so thankful that I accepted Jesus as my Lord and Savior and continue to bask in His love daily.

If you haven't ever asked Jesus to cleanse you from your sins and give you a new start, you can do that right now. You don't have to be inside a church or have a pastor lead you in a special prayer to become a Christian. You can pray right now and simply confess your sins, ask Him to forgive you, and make Him the Lord of your life. That's it! I know it sounds too good to be true, but Christ *is* the truth. Jesus adores you and longs to be your Savior, so receive His love today. Allow Him to direct your steps and lead you into the plan He has for you. I promise—it's even better than a Mrs. Fields cookie.

No Substitutions

Debora M. Coty

*Jesus said to him, "I am the way, and the truth,
and the life; no one comes to the Father but through Me."*
John 14:6 NASB

I've heard of green eggs and ham, but this is ridiculous!" my daughter leaned close and whispered, careful to keep her comments out of earshot of our extended family gathered around the Thanksgiving table.

She was referring to the huge, nearly untouched dish of what was supposed to be sweet potato casserole. Topped with a delicious mixture of chopped pecans, coconut, and brown sugar, creamed sweet potatoes were a favorite at our family holiday celebrations.

But something was definitely amiss this year. Instead of their usually inviting orangey sweetness, the potatoes were pea green. My sister, the chronically distracted cook, had reached into the cabinet for vanilla extract and grabbed the similarly shaped bottle of green food coloring instead.

By the time she'd realized her mistake, it was too late. "Well, they may look different, but they'll taste the same," she reasoned as she popped the casserole dish in the oven.

But it just didn't work that way. No one could bring themselves to scoop the sickly green grub onto their plates. We just couldn't wrap our heads—or appetites—around a substitute for the real thing.

I experienced a similar experience while, in the throes of a strict diet, I was hosting a dinner party. At a quandary about what to serve for dessert, I settled on a low-calorie pie recipe that looked simply scrumptious in the photo. All the regular cheesecake ingredients had been replaced with fat-free, sugar-free substitutes, topped with fat-free whipped topping and drizzled with zero-calorie faux chocolate sauce.

It turned out gorgeous! I was so proud to be serving my guests such a masterpiece that wouldn't add more wattle to their waddles. And I could enjoy it, too!

Amid oohs and aahs from my appreciative guests marveling at my creative culinary genius, I cut large slices and served them on my best china.

At their first bites, I saw the faces all around me fall. Everyone suddenly found their shoes extremely interesting as I sampled my lovely pie. Yucko! It tasted like soggy cardboard. Magazine-cover beautiful it might have been, but as we scraped most of the pie into the disposal, we all agreed there's no substitute for the real thing.

At least I was able to laugh about my culinary faux pas, but it made me think. Faith can be like that pie. Many religions look tempting on the outside, but once you get past the fluffy frosting, you find the ingredients have no real substance. They're inferior. Flat. Fake.

Jesus made it very clear that true faith is found only through Him.

He, Himself, *is* truth. And the *only* way to a living, breathing, dynamic relationship with Papa God is through Jesus. Everything else is just a poor substitute for the real thing.

As worthless in the end as faux cheesecake.

CH-CH-CH-CH-CH-CHANGES

MICHELLE MEDLOCK ADAMS

"I the LORD do not change."
MALACHI 3:6 NIV

I am impulsive. I get excited pretty easily and jump in with both feet—not always a good quality. So, when I read on a magazine cover, "Eat a can of pineapple before you go to bed and speed up your metabolism!" the first thing I did was run to the store, purchase ten cans of pineapple juice, and begin downing a can before bed each night. Of course I didn't lose any weight, and all of that acidic pineapple left my mouth with small blisters. Later, I read that drinking a spoonful of apple cider vinegar before every meal would promote better health and weight loss. The verdict is still out on that one. . .I'll let you know. Just recently, I saw a news report touting the amazing weight-loss benefits of Wu-Long tea, so I am wondering if I should order some of that, too.

It seems that every single day a new-and-improved product will come out and claim to be a great aid in promoting weight loss. Or a new study will pop up and reveal what we once thought was a good vitamin to aid in body fat reduction is actually harmful to one's health. Who knew? Obviously, things change. New information is discovered. New studies emerge. New products are invented. Sometimes, it seems almost impossible to keep up with current trends and teaching and differentiate between truth and myth.

Aren't you glad that God never changes? I am so thankful that the Bible says God is the same yesterday, today, and forever. I am so thankful that I won't wake up tomorrow and discover that grace is no longer available to me or that prayer only works on Tuesdays. In a world that changes every minute, God is my stability, my rock, my love, and my foundation. His love is never ending. And His mercies are new every morning. We can totally rely on Him and trust His Word— no matter what. Isn't that comforting?

So, if you're feeling a little frazzled with all of the stuff going on in the world or you're tired of hearing about the latest, greatest exercise gadget, spend some quality time with your Father. Let Him reassure you of who you are in Him and surround you with His unconditional love. You'll come away from that time with Him completely refreshed and ready to face the day. Now, I've got to run. . .the Fed Ex guy is here with my order of Wu-Long tea.

FOOD FOR THOUGHT: GOD'S WORD

If you have formed the habit of checking on every new diet that comes along, you will find that, mercifully, they all blur together, leaving you with only one definite piece of information: french-fried potatoes are out.

JEAN KERR

TIPS FROM THE MASTERS

JANICE HANNA

*Each one should test their own actions. Then they can
take pride in themselves, alone, without comparing themselves
to someone else, for each one should carry their own load.*
GALATIANS 6:4–5 NIV

I have many (formerly chubby) friends who consider themselves professional dieters, so I went to them for advice, wondering if they could help me shave off a few pounds. One of them told me to buy a bigger purse. Apparently carrying a bigger purse makes you look smaller. She went on to tell me that she did her purse shopping in the luggage department. Another told me to add salsa to my tuna fish instead of mayo. (Ack! Where's the fun in that?) Yet another reminded me to drink more water. (I can now tell you where every bathroom in town is located.)

My mother advised me never go to the grocery store on an empty stomach. (Please don't tell her that I filled up on fast food before buying this week's groceries.) My father's plan: When you go out to eat, only consume half of what's on your plate. (Whatever happened to our parents telling us to clean our plates?) A good friend advised me to prepare meals in advance so I wouldn't be tempted to go out to eat. (You should see my freezer. I couldn't squeeze anything else in there if I tried.)

Oy! How I've struggled when it comes to figuring out this dieting thing. A peek inside my closet will give you all the proof you need. It's filled with clothes in every size. Why? Because, over the past ten years or so, I've actually *been* every size. Up, down, around and around. . .I feel like a yo-yo. In spite of all the great advice I'm getting from friends and family, nothing seems to be helping in the long-term. Could it be that the real problem is mine to fix, not theirs?

Yep. All of their ideas are well and good, but none of them will make a bit of difference until I make up my mind not to waver. And though my friends all have their own personal plans, I have to remember that what works for them won't necessarily work for me. Sure, I can consider their advice—good, bad, and otherwise—and pray about it. I can try the things that make sense. But in the end, I have to settle on a personal plan of action and stick with it. Otherwise, this vicious cycle will continue.

What about you? Do you spend too much time asking others what works for them? Do you talk about dieting but never actually do it? If so, maybe it's time to skip the advice and just cut back on what you're eating. Take the dog for a walk. Put less butter on the popcorn. And while you're at it, why not go to the real Master when you're unsure of what to do? The Bible is loaded with great tidbits to help you overcome temptation. It will give you plenty of food for thought, all of it calorie- and carb-free. And you won't even have to buy a bigger purse!

No More Weeds
in the Lettuce Salad

Tina Krause

*"The kingdom of heaven is like a man who sowed good seed
in his field. But while everyone was sleeping, his enemy
came and sowed weeds among the wheat. . . . When the wheat
sprouted and formed heads, then the weeds also appeared."*

Matthew 13:24–26 niv

There comes a time in every dieter's life when we yearn to toss our low-fat soups and salads into the sea of reckless abandon. I'm at that point now. After weeks of watching what I eat, I want to eat what I watch—whipped cream pies and foods that start with the letter *f*—namely, fried chicken, french fries, and fried veggies served in one of those baskets lined in translucent paper where pools of grease puddle at the bottom.

But tipping the scale at an unmentionable weight has frightened me enough to load my grocery cart with low-fat cottage cheese, wheat bran, and dark leafy greens, as I peruse books on full-body cleanses guaranteed to detoxify by dissolving my fat like Metamucil in water.

"I mean it, Jim," I announce with the earnestness of a reformed drug addict. "I refuse to eat 'that stuff' again."

"That stuff?" asks my husband.

"Yep, the stuff that turned this once fit body into a life-size blob of Silly Putty!"

I remember my former days of fitness (way back when). My heart-healthy lifestyle consisted of jogging twenty-five miles a week and eating sensibly. Doing so kept the pounds off for many years. Back then, I welcomed unexpected sightings of people I hadn't seen in years because I could flaunt my fit physique and bask in the flow of their compliments. Today, I duck behind boxes of Twinkies in the grocery store, hoping no one will notice me.

Of course, I have valid reasons for my weight gain. Here are a few favorites:

- Too little time and too tired to exercise consistently.

- Junk food is quicker and easier to make.

- Stress. (My mantra? When in stress, reach for a plate of double chocolate chip cookies.)

- Aging. (I always hated the as-you-get-older-it's-harder-to-take-the-weight-off excuse. Now, unlike my clothing, it fits me well.)

Interestingly, my reasons for not doing what I know I should spill over into my spiritual life, too. Though my intentions are good, I allow daily intrusions to rob me from spending time with God. Read my Bible? Maybe later after I finish my work. Quiet prayer time? I'm too tired now; I need some sleep.

Excuses spring up faster than weeds after a summer rain. Sounds similar to a parable Jesus gave. He said that the weeds of sin, worldly preoccupations, and lame excuses choke the seed of God's Word in our hearts. As a result, we become weakened, unproductive, and fruitless. In moments of weakness I have ignored the still small voice within. But not anymore.

"Yep, Jim, I'm staying with the program," I say, reinforcing my resolve. "No more excuses."

"What program?" hubby asks from somewhere in oblivion.

"You know, my *diet*?" I snarl. "No more weeds in the lettuce salad for me!"

Confused, my husband exits. But I'm staying with the good seed of God's Word exclusively, even if that includes a full-body cleanse.

Mirrors

Tina Krause

*But we all with unveiled face, beholding as in a mirror
the glory of the Lord, are being transformed into the same
image from glory to glory just as from the Lord, the Spirit.*
2 Corinthians 3:18 nasb

Health clubs use a picture-is-worth-a-thousand-words philosophy. Their technique? Mirrors everywhere. From the locker room to the weight room, one cannot escape one's reflection. Whole walls are dedicated to reveal the truth of one's physical condition.

Recently, I visited a local health club. Since I've gained a few pounds (okay, more than a few), the idea of sweating and straining seemed reasonable.

My first session of step aerobics was a lesson in life. The employee, who resembled the cover girl of a fitness magazine, escorted me to the aerobics room with its solid wall of floor-to-ceiling mirrors. Standing face-to-face with my bigger-than-life imperfect body was bad enough.

But forced to compare my flaws with the long-legged leotard beauties that surrounded me was cruel. They looked as if they indulged in step aerobics like I indulge in hot fudge sundaes.

In a room flaunting Spandex and firm thighs, I stood out like a Denise Austin reject in my loose sweatpants and oversize T-shirt. The twenty other people in the room needed a workout about as much as I needed another chocolate bonbon.

As the upbeat music blared, the instructor shouted, "March in place! Right foot step changes!" I concentrated intensely on following the lead of the svelte exercise enthusiast in front of me, who acted as if she had the lung capacity to run ten miles while humming the *Rocky* theme song.

Forty minutes later, the mirrors revealed my true identity. Red faced and clumsy, I stumbled to synchronize the step changes with the arm movements. As the session intensified, everyone counted aloud while the instructor issued commands in a marching-cadence manner: "Up, up, tap down. Left leg, turn and tap." She might have well been speaking Swahili; and for a moment I thought the class required tap shoes. Meanwhile, I stared at the face and body of a woman in desperate need of pulmonary resuscitation.

So I've concluded that mirrors accomplish one of two things: challenge us to realize our need to visit the health club more often or humiliate the fatties among us, thereby eliminating baggy sweats from the premises completely.

The Bible works much the same way as the mirror of God's Word reflects our true image. The truth of who we are will either challenge us or drive us away. The choice is ours.

At first we may feel embarrassed and clumsy as everyone else appears more conditioned, flexing their spiritual muscles. But God is a kind and patient instructor who welcomes those weighed down by sin to see them through to spiritual fitness. With God, sweatpants transform into Spandex if we will only face our imperfect reflections.

Mirrors aren't so bad after all. So bring them on, I'm ready for some spiritual conditioning. . .and maybe even another step aerobics class.

CHOCOLATE—
THE FLAVOR OF MY LIFE

MICHELLE MEDLOCK ADAMS

When your words came, I ate them;
they were my joy and my heart's delight.
JEREMIAH 15:16 NIV

I pushed through the crowd of other ponytailed girls for a glimpse at *...the list*. It had been four hours since freshman cheerleading tryouts, and now was the moment of truth. Out of sixty-four girls vying for six spots on the Bedford North Lawrence High School Freshman Cheer Team, had I made it? My eyes scanned each number—*where's 23?* I looked down at the number on my chest, just to make sure it didn't match any of the six numbers on the list, but I already knew the answer. I hadn't made the squad. I'd been cheerleader in fifth, sixth, seventh, and eighth grade, but I'd have to sit on the sidelines my freshman year of high school. I felt like I'd been run over by a huge truck, which then backed up over me. I congratulated the girls in the corner who were already celebrating their accomplishment of making the squad, and then I walked out the gym door toward Mom's car. She'd been waiting patiently. It was one of the longest walks of my life.

Before I could utter the words, "I didn't make it," she already knew.

Mom didn't say a word; she just reached over and hugged me. As we drove home, the car was silent except for the short bursts of sobbing coming from my side of the car. Then she stopped the car in downtown Bedford.

"What are you doing?" I asked, wiping the mascara from my face.

"I'll be right back," she said, then hustled into a nearby store.

When Mom returned, she had a bag from Hoover's Candy Store. She handed it to me and said, "Go ahead. Dig in! Life is too short to be sad."

I smiled as I peered into the little white paper bag to find double-dipped chocolate-covered peanuts—my all-time favorite candy in the world!

"Thanks," I said, while biting into my first double-dipped delicacy.

And so the tradition began. Anytime there was something in life to get over or something in life to celebrate—we did it with chocolate. We didn't overdo it. A truffle here. A turtle there. But the tradition remained strong throughout my life.

During my senior year, when I decided to try out for cheerleader again and made the varsity squad, we drove straight to Hoover's Candy Shop and celebrated with—you guessed it—double-dipped chocolate-covered peanuts. When Mom won the city golf tournament, we split a chocolate dessert called "death by chocolate" at a nearby restaurant.

Now that I'm in my forties, a turtle here and a truffle there tend to end up on my thighs, so I've had to find other ways of coping and celebrating. I've learned that God's Word is full of truffles of goodness and turtles of promise. No matter whether I'm sad from a loss or elated over a victory, I can savor every tidbit of truth in my Bible, and Mom's words still apply: "Go ahead. Dig in! Life is too short to be sad."

A True Cleanse

Michelle Medlock Adams

Create in me a clean heart, O God.
Psalm 51:10 NKJV

As I forced down another gulp of the putrid mixture of cayenne pepper, lemon juice, and maple syrup, I ran to the kitchen sink in case I wouldn't be able to swallow the horrible concoction. But I did it!

"Whew, one bottle down, four more to go," I announced, quite proudly.

"Why are you doing this again?" my husband asked, glancing over the top of the newspaper he was reading.

"It's a cleanse. . .supposed to be really healthy for you," I explained, while making another magical mixture to drink later that afternoon.

"So it's a health thing, not a weight-loss thing, then," he insinuated.

"Well. . ." I paused, trying to choose my words carefully. "There are many benefits to a cleanse of this type and, yes, losing weight is one of those benefits."

"That's what I thought," he said smugly.

Since I was already busted, I figured I might as well come clean, so I added, "And Beyonce lost like ten pounds in three days doing this exact cleanse, so I thought I'd try it."

Of course my husband knew there had to be some weight-loss benefit at the end of the horrible cleanse rainbow or I wouldn't be the least bit interested. He knows me too well. Over our twenty years of marriage, he has seen me try just about every weight-loss gimmick, gadget, and diet known to man or woman. I'm always on the mission to lose those "last ten pounds." Can I get an amen? Sure, I know that a healthy diet and a consistent exercise program are key to losing weight and keeping it off, but those two things combined never seem to produce the weight-loss results quickly enough for me. Thus, I buy into the promises of "Lose weight while you sleep!" and "30 pounds in 30 days for 30 dollars." If I had all the money spent on those thirty-dollar magic pills and potions that I've tried over the years, I would be a wealthy woman.

So why do we do it? Why do women all over the world try all these crazy concoctions and gimmicky exercise gadgets to lose weight? I think it all boils down to this: We are desperate for results. We'd do anything for something that will work—even if it means gagging as we drink a putrid mixture of cayenne pepper, lemon juice, and maple syrup.

Just think if we all became that desperate for God. . . .

Just think if we invested that same energy and had that same intense passion for God's Word that we do for the latest studies on diet pill X. . . .

It's so easy to get wrapped up in superficial things when all the while, God is beckoning us to spend time with Him. He designed our bodies and He knows how they work. And, yes, He will be our helpmate as we fight that good fight of faith in the battle of the bulge. And let's face it; feasting on His Word tastes much better than cayenne pepper, lemon juice, and maple syrup.

"Go for the Burn"

Michelle Medlock Adams

"Come to me, all you who are weary and burdened,
and I will give you rest. Take my yoke upon you and learn from me,
for I am gentle and humble in heart, and you will find rest for
your souls. For my yoke is easy and my burden is light."
MATTHEW 11:28–30 NIV

I have always been somewhat of a fitness junkie. It wasn't that I wanted to have the lowest resting heart rate or the ability to run the fastest mile. I just wanted to fit into my jeans with ease. In high school, I remember starting my days doing Jane Fonda's workout—leg warmers, leotard, headband, and all. Every morning, I'd hear her coaching, "Go for the burn! Go for the burn!" So I did. I went for the burn. I wasn't exactly sure what "the burn" was, but I was pretty sure it had something to do with intense pain. Thus, I grew up in the aerobics-era way of thinking: If it doesn't hurt, it must not be working.

After I became a certified fitness instructor in college, I learned there was a difference between *pushing* yourself and *hurting* yourself. Pushing yourself means going another mile on the treadmill when it's easier to stop after just one mile. Hurting yourself means continuing to jog when sharp pains are shooting through your joints. There is a distinct difference, and as you begin to know your body, you learn the difference between "the burn" and "intense pain." Going for the burn has a good end result, whereas pushing yourself to the point of pain only results in injury.

I've learned that same principle applies to our spiritual walk. God wants us to dive into His Word and allow Him to change us and become more like Him. During those growing times, we might experience some of "the burn" of growing pains, but it's a good pain. It's a good burn because God is reshaping us and molding us and taking us to another level. That is totally different than trying to carry all the weight of the world on our shoulders and bear the burdens that Jesus already bore for us on the cross at Calvary more than two thousand years ago. God doesn't want us to endure the pain His Son already went through on our behalf. That whole concept of "suffering for Jesus" is simply not biblical or productive in our Christian lives. Jesus suffered so we wouldn't have to—He took our place.

So, go for the burn, spiritually speaking, but don't take on the pain that Jesus already withstood on your behalf. Instead, praise Him for bearing your burdens! And if you want to go for the burn wearing leg warmers, a leotard, and a headband? Even better.

DIETING IS NO CAKEWALK:
TEMPTATION

It is a hard matter, my fellow citizens,
to argue with the belly, since it has no ears.
PLUTARCH

THE SECRET TO WEIGHT LOSS AND OTHER MYTHS

TINA KRAUSE

Wherein ye greatly rejoice, though now for a season, if need be,
ye are in heaviness through manifold temptations.
1 PETER 1:6 KJV

Most people have engaged in the battle of the bulge at one time or another in their lifetime. Admit it, who among us hasn't sought the ultimate secret to conquering flabby thighs and tubby tummies?

I'm one of those seekers of slimness. In fact, I have dieted on and off most, if not all, of my adult life. As a result, I consider myself a diet guru, qualified to offer some pound, er, *sound* advice. From the mouth of one who has consumed enough food to find herself in a lard-laden state, I have gleaned some weight-loss observations on my quest for thinness. So here is my skinny on dieting:

• If it tastes good, spit it out.

- The older you get, the harder it is to lose weight because your body and fat have become long-time friends and it's hard to separate best buddies.

- Dieting is not a piece of cake. . .nor is it a cakewalk.

- When at first you don't succeed, di-diet again.

- Cravings are just our body's way of telling us that it's having no fun.

Okay, maybe these diet observations are less than sound, but who can dispute their credibility? Truth is, the journey down the dieter's road is laden with tempting trails, fattening foods, and enticing eateries. These are the not-so-pleasingly plump potholes that flatten our tires—except the spare ones around the middle—sabotaging our good intentions.

The above scripture encourages us to rejoice when temptations, food-related or otherwise, cross our pathways. Temptations present us with the opportunity to exercise our faith and determination to choose right over wrong, or rutabaga over rigatoni.

In the same way that we resist, ignore, and reject spiritual temptations in our lives, we must exercise (literally) the same willpower toward fatty foods and a lazy lifestyle. So, with that in mind, here are some better suggestions that just might help!

- Pace yourself. A hearty savings account takes time to accumulate, much like a hefty deposit of fat to the hips. Exercise patience (physically and spiritually) and give yourself time.

- Be consistent and persistent. Count and record daily calories, and if you fall off the wagon, waddle back on and keep moving forward!

- Allow for mistakes and breaks. Hey, no one is perfect! Allow yourself a treat once in a while. (The key words being *once* and *in a while*!)

Discovering the ultimate diet secret that will melt pounds faster than ice cream in the summer sun is a myth. We all want instant results, but results take time. Much like our spiritual walk, we must take one day at a time as we resist temptations, seek the Lord, exercise our faith (and sagging muscles), and make right choices. Before long, our spirits will grow as our waistlines shrink!

SECRET SNATCHING PRODUCES WEIGHTY WARDROBE

TINA KRAUSE

*Thou hast set our iniquities before thee,
our secret sins in the light of thy countenance.*
PSALM 90:8 KJV

Trays of goodies lined the table at a bridal shower I attended. But I stuck to my diet. "No thanks," I said as someone passed me a plate of homemade brownies. "I'm dieting."

"Oh, you've got to try this. One won't hurt," the hostess assured me. But I resisted, even though I could easily eat chocolate anything in one swooping gulp. By the end of the evening, my dietary restrictions were common knowledge as I refused one delectable after another.

By the time I returned home, however, visions of double-chocolate cake danced in my head as I stood in the kitchen, alone. *No cake, but we do have chocolate chip cookies,* I thought. *I haven't eaten since lunch, so certainly one is okay.*

Gingerly, I lifted the lid off the cookie jar so no one in the house could hear me. Snatching a few cookies, I poured a glass of skim milk and hurriedly downed all of it in a matter of seconds. As I brushed the crumbs from the table, my husband entered.

"What are you doing?"

Like a cat swallowing a goldfish, I wiped my mouth with the back of my hand and tried to appear innocent. "Nothing. . .why?" I stammered.

"I just wondered," he said with a shrug and exited the kitchen.

Whew, I pulled it off. Or so I thought. That was months ago, and I haven't lost a pound since. In fact, sneaking a few forbidden foods have gradually added, not subtracted, bulky inches to my hips.

My lack of results reminds me of what I already know—what I do in secret will eventually be exposed in the light of day. Some say that we are what we eat, but I tout a different philosophy; namely, we *wear* what we eat. Thus, I now wear the weighty wardrobe of too many cookies, cakes, and pasta for all the world to see.

Someone wisely stated, "You are only what you are when no one is looking." That holds true from a spiritual perspective as well. Unless we walk the spiritual talk, we deceive ourselves. In fact, secret sins are much like secret eating. Both hurt us and have the potential to damage our testimony.

So I've concluded that my secret snatching is over, and I'm dieting again. This time, with God's help, I'll make it. How will you know? Check out what I'm wearing six months from now.

THE VOICE OF CHOICE

JANET ROCKEY

When the woman saw that the tree was good for food. . .
she took from its fruit and ate.

GENESIS 3:6 NASB

Looking at the array of desserts at a church function, I spied a cheesecake topped with miniature chocolate brownies. *Remember what the doctor said about your blood sugar,* I said to myself.

The doctor said it wasn't diabetic *high, just a bit elevated,* the wicked voice whispered in my left ear. *You surely shall not die.*

I countered with a scripture verse. "Get behind me, Satan."

Hmm, Wicked murmured, *it looks even more delicious from back here.*

I almost caved.

No, the wise voice countered in my right ear. *What nutritional value does it offer?*

"None," I answered. I backed away with renewed confidence and headed toward the beverage table. God always provides a means for escape.

The unrelenting wicked voice followed me. *If God doesn't want you to have sweets, then all the desserts will be gone when you come back.*

How I detest that wicked voice. It always makes sense at the time, but returns to taunt me when I submit to it. *Now see what you've done, you weakling. Look at your disgusting fat belly! Oh, your aching joints. It's the sugar, you know.* So smug.

After chatting with a few friends, I ambled back by the table of temptation. All the desserts were gone. Except one.

Wicked changed its tone to sound like a piece of cheesecake topped with miniature chocolate brownies. *Poor me,* it cried, *no one wants me. I'm so lonely. Have pity on me.*

Walk away, Wise whispered. *Just walk away.*

I tried to walk away, but Wicked was so convincing. *God must want you to have that piece of cheesecake, or it wouldn't be waiting for you.*

Like Eve in the garden, I yielded. My weakness didn't affect the fall of mankind, only my struggle to develop healthy eating habits. God provided a means of escape, but I listened to the wrong voice. No diabetic coma ensued. My waistline didn't immediately expand. The button didn't pop off my skirt. The seams didn't rip open. The consequences of caving to temptation aren't always instantaneous. But the cheesecake topped with miniature chocolate brownies didn't taste as delicious as I expected. Unsatisfied, I tossed the half-eaten dessert into the trash can.

Of course Wicked rebuked me, not only about eating the cheesecake, but also for wasting perfectly good food.

Wise consoled me. *You'll be stronger next time.*

I've prayed for God to remove all temptation from me. But He uses challenges to develop the strength of character He wants me to have. Sometimes I fail, but often I succeed. Although my failures attempt to weaken my resolve, I grow stronger with each success. God's grace is sufficient for me.

Chocolate for Lunch

Meredith LeBlanc

*"Keep watching and praying that you may not come into temptation;
the spirit is willing, but the flesh is weak."*

Mark 14:38 NASB

February in Indiana is gray and dismal. Not the best weather to lift one's spirits, especially with a milestone birthday looming. Mix in depravation of comfort foods to comply with a rigorous diet, and you have a nasty concoction of depression.

It's time to call Janelle, a friend from my Bible study group.

"Hi, Janelle, how's the diet going?"

"Must we talk about diets? I am sick of carrot sticks and celery," she said.

"I feel the same way! Actually, I called to ask you about that candy shop you mentioned at Bible study last week."

"Meredith, I don't think that's a safe subject either."

"I know, but hear me out. You have a birthday this month, right?"

"Yes, and so do you. What does that have to do with diets and candy shops?"

"I wanted to ask you to have lunch with me to celebrate our birthdays."

"Okay, that sounds like fun. What do you have in mind?"

"First let me tell you about this article I read concerning the health benefits of chocolate. Eating chocolate increases the levels of endorphins released into the brain. The endorphins lessen pain and decrease stress."

"Oh no, I think I see where you are going with this. I am not so sure this is going to be your best idea."

"Let me finish. The article went on to say that chocolate also affects our levels of serotonin, an antidepressant. You know we need an antidepressant. What better way to get it than by eating chocolate? Chocolate is a natural food and so much better than taking Prozac. Janelle, birthdays only come once a year. Let's go to the candy shop and treat ourselves to an afternoon of bliss."

"Meredith, this is not normal."

"You know what they say about normal? 'Normal is nothing more than a cycle on a washing machine.' Come on, Janelle, what's the risk?"

We set the date for the next Monday. I had a prudent breakfast in anticipation of the lavish lunch of sweet milk chocolate, dark bitter chocolate, creamy white chocolate, served plain, cream filled, decorated, laden with a variety of nuts.

At the shop we peruse the display before us, carefully making our choices. Time is of no consequence. We enjoy each luscious piece. Janelle identifies each piece and describes the complexity of that particular creation. It is a time of complete self-indulgence.

The guilt sets in on the way home. "Feasting on chocolate is not as much fun as I thought it would be," Janelle said.

"The next time I tempt you, remind me to pray to resist my weak nature."

Many times I have joked about my spirit being willing but my flesh is weak. Now I know the rest of the story. The words before that phrase are the key for us. It is necessary to keep a watch for times in our lives that temptation is upon us. The solution, of course, is to resist temptation. God is our strength.

WHERE THE TASTE BEGINS

VALORIE QUESENBERRY

If I regard iniquity in my heart, the Lord will not hear.
PSALM 66:18 NKJV

We dieters love "free" foods. Those are the ones you're supposed to be able to eat without paying for them later on the scales. They're the ones that are empty of fat, sodium, calories, and, sometimes, flavor. The point is that you can enjoy pleasure without guilt. At least, that's what the advertisers tell us on packages and in commercials. Eat these cookies or this gelatin dessert and you can treat your taste buds to no-worry indulgence. You get all the flavor, but none of the calories! You avoid the price of indulgence. And there is always an accompanying image of a svelte woman laughingly enjoying the snack. The message is strong: Eat this dessert and you can avoid the usual calorie cost. And the message is powerful; the sales prove it. (Though, come to think of it, I rarely see real-life dieters smiling as they indulge in fat-free, low-carb, non-hydrogenated, oil-laden goodies! It's really difficult to believe that this free food is just as good as the real thing!)

Satan uses that free-food line on us in many other ways. But, unfortunately, he doesn't have our betterment in mind. Rather, his intent is to deceive. He attempts to pull us into sin by promising that we won't have to pay the price. In fact, often he just wants to get us thinking about yielding, considering what giving in would be like.

He swirls the image in our minds, pushing us to imagine its taste, much like a dieter contemplating a forbidden bite of chocolate. He tells us we don't even need to swallow, just savor the thought for a while, enjoying the "free" flavor. He knows somewhere along that path, the battle will be decided in the mind.

The word *regard* in the original language of Psalm 66:18 has the meaning of "to look at, inspect, perceive, or consider." The psalmist was saying that even savoring the thought of sin in the heart can interrupt one's connection with God. What takes place in the mind follows in reality. And the consequences are anything but guilt-free.

Oh, how many wonderful diets have been sabotaged by wandering thoughts! If I allow visions of chocolate truffles and french fries to parade gleefully through my head, it is certain that my actions will follow my thinking. Thankfully, the consequences of succumbing to a bonbon aren't tragic, but if I desire success in my quest for a thinner me, I really ought to pay attention to what I savor in my mind. Because once I imagine its taste, I'm a goner. At least, that's how it works with me.

Say "No, No" to Yo-Yo!

Michelle Medlock Adams

But since you are lukewarm and neither cold nor hot,
I will spit you out of my mouth.
Revelation 3:16 cev

Dictionary.com defines *yo-yo dieting* as "the practice of repeatedly losing weight by dieting and subsequently regaining it." It might have been easier for Dictionary.com to just put my picture next to that definition. Truly, I have lost and gained the same ten pounds about a dozen times in my life. And it seems I am not alone. Statistics reveal that 80 percent of the people who lose weight will regain it after two years.

Not very encouraging, is it? Yo-yo dieting isn't only frustrating, but it's dangerous for your health. Studies reveal that the vicious cycle of losing weight and regaining it can result in high blood pressure, high cholesterol, cancer, diabetes, and depression. So, why do we fall back into the same patterns that caused us to gain weight in the first place?

It doesn't make any sense at all, yet many of us drift back into those unhealthy habits and the weight slowly returns.

Experts say that until you identify the stressors or triggers that cause you to regain the weight, you'll never be able to keep it off. For instance, I have identified a few "trigger foods" (tasty morsels that set me off on an eating binge) that I simply will not allow in my house. Why? Because I know if I buy a bag of those little white powdered doughnuts, I won't eat just one or two. No, I'll finish the whole bag in one sitting. I have no restraint when it comes to those powdery pieces of heaven, so I don't keep them in my house. And when it's close to Easter and those Reese's peanut butter eggs make their debut in the supermarket, I almost run over other shoppers in an attempt to run away from those yummy treats. Why? Because if I buy a box of six, I'll eat two on the way home from the supermarket and probably finish off the rest before bedtime. I know my trigger foods.

I've also come to know my trigger sins when it comes to my Christian walk. One of my trigger sins is allowing myself to become too busy. Yes, being too busy is the "powdered sugar doughnuts" and "Reese's peanut butter eggs" in my spiritual life. I am comfortable being really busy. In fact, I thrive on it. But I end up neglecting quality time with my Lord, which is just not acceptable. If you don't know what your trigger sins are, ask God to help you identify them and deal with them so that you won't fall into a yo-yo pattern in your Christian life. And, if those little white powdered sugar doughnuts aren't a trigger food for you, enjoy a couple in my honor. Ugh!

CLEAN HOUSE OF DUST
AND DELECTABLES

TINA KRAUSE

Who can understand his errors? Cleanse thou me from secret faults.
PSALM 19:12 KJV

Pizza, potato chips, and Pepsi cans litter my kitchen counter and dining room table after my grandkids' visit. I look in the pantry, and chewy cookies lock me in a stare like a security guard at Bloomingdale's. I turn on the television and salivate during commercials laden with scenes of sizzling burgers and tempting treats. And I wonder, *Is this diet possible?*

My mind temporarily drifts to another time. It was the first warm evening of the year, so I hauled the fan from the closet and positioned it in front of my bed. (During and after menopause, staying cool is another struggle right in step with the battle of the bulge. But I digress.)

As I sat in bed reading, tiny dust balls drifted through the air in my direction. Puzzled, I investigated the area with a watchful eye, much like my stare downs of cookies in the pantry. Curious, I stood on the mattress to examine the top of my canopy bed. Ah-ha the culprit. Dust—lots of it—blanketed the wood rim that a dust cloth hadn't touched in months. Okay, maybe years.

I was oblivious to the powdery layers until the dust hit the fan and drifted all over the place. The incident catapulted me into a cleaning frenzy, wiping out all traces of dust bunnies not only at the top of the bed rim but on the blinds, under the bed, above the door trim and behind the dresser and nightstands that also house miscellaneous items like Lego pieces and paper clips.

What does this story have to do with my dieting dilemma? Two words: *Clean house.* When the pant legs of the slacks we once wore could now be cut into shirt sleeves, it's time to clear out the culinary clutter.

Similarly, the carnal clutter of bad attitudes and crummy habits blanket the hidden places of our heart until something happens to scatter and expose the dirt. God then gives us a choice to remain clueless or take action and clean our spiritual abodes. I don't know about you, but I'd rather expose the dust so that God can clean the clutter.

Determined, I'm cleaning out my cupboards and turning a blind eye to enticing food ads. Yep, the "dirt" on my diet dilemma just hit the fan.

I Fought the Law, but the Law Won

Janet Rockey

*"Do not think that I came to abolish the Law or the Prophets;
I did not come to abolish but to fulfill."*
Matthew 5:17 nasb

I recently came across old photos from my honeymoon as a young bride. Gasp! Who's that young woman in the bikini? I was slender before the Law came after me. The Law of Gravity, that is. It stalked me with the stealth of a bounty hunter.

Newton's law of gravity states things tend to fall. When he watched an apple drop to the ground, I'm sure he didn't consider gravity's impact on our body parts. Only a woman would think of that. Gravitational force exists between all objects possessing mass. The earth attracts my body part, and my body part attracts the earth with equal force. My body part moves downward because it's lighter. And that's a good thing.

I wouldn't want my added weight to move the earth.

Gravity's pull provided food for thought (pun intended) as I squared off with a plate of brownies. My body has mass. Brownies have mass. So the brownies, which weigh less, should be pulled toward me since I weigh more. Instead, I'm going after the brownies. Can a physicist explain that paradox?

Eating the brownies increases my mass and provides more for gravity to pull. If I drop a few pounds, I'll have less mass. The gravitational pull toward the brownie should be weakened.

Or not.

If I eat healthy foods in smaller portions, I might drop excess weight. But brownies will always tempt me, triggering my spiral into the bottomless pit of dieting. Whether my scale reads a hundred and ten pounds or two hundred, the weight of temptation will remain.

I can exercise to tone and strengthen my muscles, but even the most disciplined bodybuilder wrestles with gravity's irresistible force.

History credits Isaac Newton with the discovery of the laws of gravity, but almighty God set them in place when He created the world.

I tossed that old photograph aside, realizing I'll never be that size or shape again. Some things, like age and gravity, are irreversible. I can cope with the law of gravity, knowing that a spiritual force tugs at my heart, drawing me closer to God's everlasting love.

CALMING THE MILKSHAKES:
PEACE IN THE PROCESS

Inside some of us is a thin person struggling to get out,
but they can usually be sedated with a few pieces of chocolate cake.
UNKNOWN

FALLING FROM THE
CARROT PEDESTAL

JO RUSSELL

Cast all your anxiety on him because he cares for you.
1 PETER 5:7 NIV

After a life-threatening crisis, I lost forty pounds and kept it off for nearly a decade. Then I embraced a healthy lifestyle. I didn't let anyone forget it. I chimed out advice, whether someone wanted to hear it or not.

"To lose weight, drink more water; eat more veggies, less bread, and fewer carbs." I'd finish with the battle cry, "Most of all, remember that fried foods are three times the calories!"

At potlucks, I'd let it all out:

"Ice cream? Pure chemical poisoning!"

"Cookies with frosting? Never!"

"A soda? One can has thirteen spoonfuls of sugar!"

It's a wonder someone didn't clobber me with a slow cooker.

Any person is bound to fall from that kind of pedestal. A seven-year-old named Katie took me down in six hours.

Though I watched my portions, went to the gym even if it was late, and ate balanced meals, I fell off my carrot pedestal with Katie. She was a bouncy second grader with problems more flammable than dryer lint. It was my last year before retiring from a career of teaching. It took everything I had to deal with her upsets each day. Katie always ended a school day by wrapping her arms around my legs in a hug. By the end of the day, she was fine!

Not me. On really rough days, I'd travel home, thinking about chocolate frosting. Yep, that was the pure junk food made with butter, cocoa, and sugar.

Surely, I could quiet this craving with good food! I ate fruit and a dinner salad. The frosting was still calling to me. I ate cheese. Dark thick swirls flashed in my mind like a big-screen preview. I went to the gym, remembering how many laps I had to swim to work off the dressing on my salad.

It was now so late, I knew I'd be seeing Katie again in six hours. The ingredients for chocolate frosting seemed to slither out of the cupboard and seductively lie on the bed next to me. I gave in during those wee hours and ate the whole container.

By the end of the school year, my stress was at its peak. I found myself eating frosting for dinner for the third time in a week, and it wasn't even Friday. Frosting was no way to deal with stress and problems!

I needed help.

"Lord, forgive me. I know You love Katie and You love me. You'll show me more ways to help her and take care of myself. You taught me how. Together we can handle anything." I started pitching God my problems and Katie's. It helped.

That year, with God as my partner, I got back to a healthy lifestyle.

Humbled by the chocolate experience, I toned down my advice on health. It was just in time, before someone tried to clobber me with a cake pan!

THE LORD IS MY REAR GUARD

LAURA FREUDIG

*For you will not go out with haste, nor will you go in flight
[as was necessary when Israel left Egypt]; for the Lord will
go before you, and the God of Israel will be your rear guard.*

ISAIAH 52:12 AMP

Despite the awkwardness of being the only pregnant woman at the health club I belonged to, I exercised all through my fourth pregnancy. The hard-bodied twenty-year-olds that surrounded me lifted weight stacks taller than the stack of baby books by my bed, but I kept at it, thinking of the jeans I wanted to be able to squeeze back into without asphyxiating and the sweet baby I wanted to be able to chase around without gasping for breath. I thought I hadn't gained an excessive amount of weight. However, when I returned to my exercise regimen at about six weeks postpartum, the removal of an eight-and-a half-pound baby hadn't made a noticeable dent in my circumference.

As I pulled my too-tight shorts (hand-me-downs from my sister's soccer-playing days in high school and fashionably baggy on *her*) up over my squishy belly in the fitness center locker room, I remembered what my four-year-old son had said that morning as I was getting dressed.

Wide-eyed, as if he had made some astounding discovery, he said in an awed, but respectful tone, "Mommy, I think your underwear is too small for your skin." I sighed. It was all too true. Now that I thought about it, though I kept exercising, I had used my recent pregnancy as an excuse to eat enough for two *grown men*, not just a woman and a tiny, growing baby! "If it tastes good, chew it" had been my motto. Now I was wearing the "fruit."

I laced up my running shoes, flipped my hair into a ponytail, and vowed to spend an hour on the treadmill and do one hundred sit-ups and at least *one* complete push-up. Pausing by the row of sinks on the way out of the locker room, I checked my hair and straightened my shirt, got a sip of water and sighed again at my lumpy outline in the mirror. Then I turned around to check myself in the back. Now this I don't normally do, not deriving a lot of comfort from the rear view of my overweight self. But today I did. A small voice seemed to whisper, *Turn around.*

And indeed, it was quite a sight. The back seam of my ancient shorts had split open from waist to leg. Through the gaping seam, at least eight inches of threadbare white undies and recently-pregnant backside were in plain view.

After staring, open-mouthed, at myself in horror for a moment or two, I scuttled back to my locker and stuffed those shorts in my bag, choosing to go for a swim in the pool instead. (And, yes, I checked and rechecked all the seams in my bathing suit!) I swam my laps, rejoicing at the embarrassment that familiar, still, small voice had spared me. It never ceases to amaze me that, even in the little things, His eye is on the sparrow, and I know He watches me.

Watching My Weight

Laura Freudig

I consider that our present sufferings are not worth comparing with the glory that will be revealed in us. For the creation waits in eager expectation for the children of God to be revealed.

Romans 8:18–19 NIV

My mother's dear friend Mary Jane has always been a pillar of the church. She plays the piano, helps with vacation Bible school, teaches Sunday school, volunteers for the nursery, serves on committees, cleans the bathrooms, and brings the creamiest, most delicious casseroles to church potluck suppers. Yes, Mary Jane is a pillar of the church.

Tall, tubular, and heavy, she even looks rather like a pillar. A solid Corinthian column.

It isn't as if she doesn't *try* to lose weight, but events are against her. Many years before, she had enjoyed biking and had kept her weight under control by puffing up and down the hills in our small community. But the unfortunate confluence of a sharp downhill turn, loose gravel, and a speeding truck had caused a rather bad bicycle accident that shattered the bones in her right foot. She put on weight during her lengthy convalescence, and afterward she found it hard to find an exercise regimen that would work within the new constraints of her injury. Her foot ached, and standing or walking for any length of time just made it worse. Aerobics were out, walking was out, and jogging was definitely out. Stationary biking was tedious for one used to flying up and down hills with the wind in her hair (a fan on the table in front of her bike wasn't a convincing substitute), and swimming was impractical in our northern community where there was no public pool and the lakes remained frigid for all but a few weeks in August.

It was a vicious circle: The ache in her foot made it hard to exercise comfortably, which caused her to put on weight, which caused her foot to ache more under the strain of those extra pounds. After a while, she simply gave up the battle. And became architectural.

She didn't, however, become bitter about her plight. She tried to live her life in the light of eternity, and knew that her main job on this earth was not to be thin and toned but to become more like Jesus and introduce other people to Him.

Once she did join a weight-loss group with some other well-potlucked women from the church, but without exercise to rev up her metabolism, dieting was a miserable experience of slow starvation. And when your body thinks it's starving, it holds on to excess fat like a rock climber grips a cliff.

I saw her in the hallway at church and asked how it was going. She smiled, "Oh, I'm watching my weight." Then she pulled out both hands, forefingers and thumbs cocked like pistols, and growled in her best cowboy voice, "And if it moves, I'm gonna shoot!"

Sometimes, through circumstances or conditions beyond our control, we can't make the changes in our bodies that we want to. But this life is not forever. Before we know it, it will be over, and we will be with Jesus in our glorified bodies. And we will be gorgeous.

DID SOMEONE SAY DOUGHNUTS?

LAURA FREUDIG

"For there is nothing hidden which will not be revealed,
nor has anything been kept secret but that it should come to light.
If anyone has ears to hear, let him hear."

MARK 4:22–23 NKJV

In these lean economic times, even the United States military, flush with tax money and deficit spending, is looking at the scale with an eye to slimming down. Starting with its own members.

The military has long held weight and fitness requirements specifying the maximum weight that a serviceman or woman could carry, as well as the minimum number of sit-ups and push-ups that they could perform in a given amount of time, and still stay in the service. In more prosperous economic times, when the job market was not so tight and the military had to work harder to recruit and retain members, those requirements were often ignored. Now, however, the military is looking to cut costs by reducing personnel, and overweight soldiers are a prime target.

My husband, a member of the Coast Guard, is blessed with genes that still allow him to fit into the jeans he wore two decades ago in high school—good genes, as well as a long-standing penchant for healthy eating and daily exercise. He misses the maximum weight allowed for his height and bone structure by a good forty pounds. Others of his coworkers are not so lucky.

Two men in particular hadn't passed their first weight standards in October and needed to lose the weight by the next weigh-in in April or they would be "involuntarily separated" from their jobs. (That's military-speak for *fired*.) They continued with their normal doughnut and fast-food habits until the beginning of March, then reality set in— along with celery, fat-free yogurt, hour-long workouts, and gallons of water. During the last week, they ate nothing. Grouchy and half-starved, they both weighed in just under the wire.

The two made their way jubilantly back to the office they shared with my husband and laid into the feast they had prepared in anticipation of success. Doughnuts, soda, potato chips, thick deli sandwiches, and, oh yes, more doughnuts. They had been eating steadily for an hour when their boss came in with a serious look on his face.

"I'm going to need you two to weigh in again. There was some glitch in the computer system, and your results got erased," he said.

The two men paused, mouths stuffed too full to answer, doughnuts poised in midair. There was a long, tense silence.

Then their boss cracked a grin and laughed. "Just kidding, men," he said. He waved at their feast. "As you were!"

Despite what the foolish woman in Proverbs 9:17 promises, food eaten in secret is *not* sweet, and unless these two men decide, truly decide to change their lifestyles, they'll suffer the stress and anxiety of biannual weigh-ins for the rest of their careers. Similarly, when we become Christians, Bible reading, church, and prayer are not suddenly tacked on to a life that remains fundamentally unaltered. If we are truly born again in Christ, we become *new creations*. And the only true change is a change that begins in the heart.

WEDDING WEEK

MELANIE STILES

A friend is always loyal, and a brother
is born to help in time of need.
PROVERBS 17:17 NLT

I'm not a dressy sort of girl, but when my young girlfriend (who seemed more like a daughter) asked me to be her maid of honor, I could not find it in my heart to refuse. How much could it hurt to dress up for something so special? At least that is what my mind told me. . .right up to a week before the ceremony when I saw the color of the dress she expected me to wear. The thought of being the maid of honor, who looked a lot like an after-dinner mint traipsing in before the bride, was daunting. But the additional thought of being an after-dinner mint at my size was overwhelming. At this late date, there was no way to influence her mint-green scheme, so I had to do something with me—that is, my body. The unfortunate aspect of the situation was that I had only seven days to erase and re-create the candy-filled image I had painted in my mind.

At first I decided I could forego food completely that week, but by midmorning, I rescinded that thought. After all, a girl's gotta eat. So, I restricted myself severely, living on broth and crackers. Pretty soon the sounds of my own tummy grumbling threatened to disturb company meetings and woke me up from a dead sleep. I allowed salads to come aboard, but strictly lettuce and tomatoes.

I'm sure it was my body's intense need for protein that made me suddenly drive to the grocery store for the chicken breasts. And then to install a can of nuts in my desk drawer.

By the latter part of the week I held a chocolate bar above my keyboard, contemplating how many miles I would need to walk on the treadmill to make that go away. When I heard myself say chocolate was its own food group, I knew I was definitely about to lose the battle.

On the afternoon before the wedding I still wasn't seeing anything good. In desperation, I did what most females do. I called my best friend to vent and cry.

"Aww, baby," she comforted, "let me bring a few things over. We will sort this out."

She walked in with an overnight travel bag. Upon seeing my look of immense curiosity, she dumped its contents out on the bed. I had never seen so many Spandex-oriented objects in my life. I donned piece by piece as we "sorted" me out. I will spare you the details, but by the time I tried on the dress, I no longer reminded myself of something that takes bad breath away. In fact, I took my own breath away.

As I proudly walked down to the front of the church the next morning, I reflected on how foolish I had been to try and change years of bad habits in one week. But I also contemplated how God had provided a good friend and a bunch of Spandex to get me through the day!

MIND OVER PLATTER: SELF-DISCIPLINE

When I buy cookies I eat just four and throw the rest away.
But first, I spray them with Raid so I won't dig them
out of the garbage later. Be careful, though,
because that Raid really doesn't taste that bad.

JANETTE BARBER

It's Not So Cliché!

Melanie Stiles

For everything there is a season,
a time for every activity under heaven.
Ecclesiastes 3:1 NLT

I'll never forget the day a good friend lovingly asked, "Honey, are you getting a little too fluffy to wear those pants?" I knew she was far too tactful to say it like the old cliché. But every trite adage has a certain measure of truth behind it. And I had to own up to this one: I was too big for my own britches.

I quickly took the hint and embraced another cliché: mind over matter. I could steer my thoughts away from sugary treats toward the healthy food groups. If I didn't think about sweets, then they would cease to exist. I was convinced my plan would work. I could easily envision those extra pounds falling away in no time.

That evening I went out to dinner with several girlfriends. I felt a bit of tension right before I opened the menu, but it quickly passed when I found a fairly appetizing salad to order. We spent the better part of the meal laughing and talking. Our waiter approached the table with an expansive dessert tray and the oohing and aahing started. I kept my eyes on the carpet. *Out of sight, out of mind. Mind over matter.* I could get through this.

In a matter of moments, there were beautiful chocolate and vanilla adventures splayed all over our table. I desperately rummaged around in my oversize handbag for a piece of gum. My mind was having definite difficulties managing the matter in front of me.

Then there were the offers.

"Oh, Mel, you didn't get anything. I can't eat this entire sundae. Let's split it."

I was going to have to confess, but I didn't want to sound pitiful or weak.

"No thanks," I said with an almost believable smile. "Didn't I tell you? Lettuce is my new chocolate!"

Smiles and giggles were immediate.

"Good luck with that, girl. Lettuce is rabbit food."

In the weeks that followed, I truly struggled at lettuce becoming my new chocolate. I liked my new motto because it got me through a tough moment, but it was going to take more than just tossing out a few words to make it through the day. I prayed earnestly, asking God to help me embrace what was coming out of my mouth and beyond. I asked Him to help me sort it all out and He led me to information. Mind over matter included learning about what else I could eat besides salads. After all, I didn't previously exist on only chocolate either. I added one healthy replacement upon another until my daily intake was balanced. By then, most of the extra pounds had slipped away. But something else had happened. I worked so hard at convincing those around me that I convinced myself.

At my next gathering with friends, I shared a dessert to celebrate not only my lost pounds, but my new knowledge. In the end, lettuce is lettuce and chocolate is chocolate, but there is a time and place for both.

LIFE IS SWEET

ARDYTHE KOLB

The baked pieces of the grain offering you
shall offer for a sweet aroma to the LORD.
LEVITICUS 6:21 NKJV

Working near a sweet aroma can be dangerous. We owned a Christian bookstore which happened to be next door to a little convenience mart, which was very handy. We could pick up incidentals without even getting in the car.

Those incidentals included some of the yummiest cinnamon rolls I've ever tasted. We bought them for a staff meeting one morning and I was hooked. Who needs breakfast when you can get something so delicious just a few steps from the door of your business?

I'm sure they were good for me. Each bite contained some of the basic food groups. The wheat, sugar, and nuts were vegetables. There were raisins (fruit), and besides all the other nutritious ingredients, the rolls provided at least the minimum daily requirement of fat, spices, and even frosting. If we popped them in the microwave, the aroma was tantalizing. We could imagine that Momma had just pulled them from her oven. The store smelled heavenly.

In spite of the nutritional value, my body didn't respond the way I wanted it to. The rolls grew more and more obvious around my midsection. It was an era when big clothes were fashionable, which concealed the cinnamon rolls until I spotted myself in a mirror at the mall one day. *Yikes! Who is that?*

Before that, I could usually win the battle with weight issues, except when I was pregnant. Even that wouldn't have been a problem if my pesky doctors had relaxed their unrealistic demands. "You can't gain more than about two pounds a month—twenty pounds altogether." I always went to male doctors, who obviously didn't have a clue.

By the time I'd realize I was pregnant, I'd gained the nine-month maximum, so I fudged a bit at the first prenatal visit when I listed my "normal" weight. It wasn't really dishonest since *normal* can mean a variety of things. It was fortunate that we moved several times during those years and I saw a different doctor with each baby.

On the days of my appointments, I didn't eat anything until after I'd stepped on the scale at the doctor's office and endured the required lecture. "You have to stop gaining so much. It's not good for you or your baby." How did he know what my baby liked? On the way home I'd buy a package of doughnuts and devour several before I arrived at our house and had to share.

Our family was complete by the time we had the bookstore, but even though I wasn't pregnant, the sweet aroma of those cinnamon rolls was almost irresistible. I finally realized that discipline and obedience create a sweet aroma to God. He wants me to please Him and do what I can to stay healthy rather than yielding to every crazy craving. And His grace is always sufficient to help me surrender to His will.

MAKING A POINT

ARDYTHE KOLB

"They savor evil as a delicacy, roll it around on their tongues,
prolong the flavor, a dalliance in decadence."
JOB 20:12–13 MSG

I'm not big on cooking—I'd much rather eat what someone else prepares, especially at a nice restaurant.

But cooking does have advantages. Everyone knows that part of being in charge of the kitchen involves tasting. The cook has to lick the bowl to clean up cake batter or frosting, and making chocolate chip cookies demands finger licking. That can be tricky when there are young children in the home who think they should be included in that process. You have to be firm, "I'm sorry honey, but too much sugar could give you a tummy ache." It's a good idea to hide the bowl in your dishwasher until the kids are occupied elsewhere and you can finish cleaning properly.

One of my most memorable experiences in the kitchen was the day I learned to make baklava. From the first taste, it moved to the top of my favorite foods list. There are only a few items I enjoy so much I could absolutely eat till I'm sick, and baklava is right there. Besides being delicious, it's bound to be nourishing—think of the protein in three cups of nuts.

The friend who taught me to make this delicacy said, "You know, baklava is the reason there's no peace in the Middle East. Israelis say it's their recipe, Syrians claim it as theirs, and chefs in Jordan and Lebanon insist they developed it." But her husband's family is from Egypt, and he swears it was their secret that some scoundrel from one of those other countries stole generations ago. International leaders should try some new tactics for peace talks—and maybe serve baklava. Hmm. Maybe not.

Even incredibly good things have certain drawbacks. The problem with making baklava is that it's supposed to be cut in small diamond-shaped pieces, and that leaves little pointy things along the edges of the baking dish. Since I certainly don't want to serve pointy things to guests nor sell them to people at a fund-raiser, I'm forced to find another method to dispose of them. Wasting food isn't an option at our house. The only solution I've come up with is to eat them myself. Those sweet honey-crusted morsels almost melt in my mouth. I love to prolong the flavor. The biblical description, "a dalliance in decadence," seems apropos.

Then one day, while trying on clothes in a department store fitting room, all those pointy things showed up. No matter how tantalizing they'd been, wearing them around my middle wasn't pretty. When I started to return the outfits to their rack, a sales lady had the nerve to ask, "Would you like to try a larger size?" I glared at her.

Eventually I faced the truth that even though nibbling baklava isn't evil, it is wrong to satisfy my cravings so much that I'm unhealthy. A good diet helps me have the energy I need to accomplish what God has planned.

THE JUICY PIG

ARDYTHE KOLB

All things are lawful for me, but not all things are helpful;
all things are lawful for me, but not all things edify.
1 CORINTHIANS 10:23 NKJV

Restaurant names can be bizarre, and sometimes they don't sound very appetizing. Places called Bonefish Grill or Le Fou Frog don't invite me in. Why would anyone choose a name that turns people away or even turns their stomach? But when you check beyond restaurants' strange labels and taste their food, those names may forever stir delicious memories.

The Juicy Pig in Denton, Texas, is one of those places. It sat on the town square in a brick building that shared walls with a hardware store on one side and a law office on the other. The inside had a typical 1960s look. But word spread from year to year, and it was always a favorite hangout for college kids.

Cafeteria food at Texas Women's University earned a bad reputation with black-eyed peas and slimy okra as part of almost every meal.

I'm a Yankee, so the menu was not only totally foreign but downright disgusting. If you love southern cooking, please forgive me—or not—it won't change my opinion. I'm sure that food wasn't a great portrayal of the South.

Quite often, after we left the cafeteria, a few of us hiked the six blocks or so to the Juicy Pig for chicken-fried steak, mashed potatoes with gravy, and homemade dinner rolls. For dessert we couldn't resist its lemon icebox pie. Sometimes we'd buy another piece of pie to enjoy back at the dorm.

Wouldn't you think walking that distance, which must have been close to a mile for the round trip, would take care of extra calories? Well, amazing as it seemed, our clothes got tighter and tighter. Eventually we were all complaining, "I've got to lose some weight. Nothing fits right anymore."

Since we all had the same problem, we skipped dinners at the cafeteria, but that didn't seem to help much.

One of the girls said, "Hey, I have a coffeepot. We can use it to boil eggs and eat them with fresh veggies for lunch." We tried that for a while, but our egg-and-celery lunches left us starving by suppertime, when we headed to the Juicy Pig. Before long we had to shop for bigger clothes. What was going on with our metabolism?

Breakfast at the cafeteria always included grits, another dish I never developed a taste for. But with lots of butter and syrup, several sausage links, and toast with jelly, it's not bad.

We didn't set out to prove Paul's statement that just because it's lawful for us to eat whatever we want, not everything is helpful. But God graphically showed me what would happen when I didn't restrain my appetite. All that rich food was edifying all right—too much; it definitely changed my shape. So, tough as it was, eventually I had to tell my friends, "I can't keep going to the Juicy Pig every evening. Maybe I'll skip Wednesdays."

CAN I GET A WITNESS?

SHELLEY R. LEE

Now go, write it on a tablet before them and inscribe it on a scroll,
that it may serve in the time to come as a witness forever.
ISAIAH 30:8 NASB

L ike a good girl, I had entered my lunch and afternoon snack eats in
my food journal, right after my breakfast, water, and late-morning
coffee entries.

It looked like I was sitting pretty with enough food allowance for
a really satisfying supper.

So I ate and I was happy! Such glorious bread and pasta with a
sprinkling of required vegetables. After I entered the happy meal count
in my journal I remembered, with a sad twinge, the handful of gummi
bears I had eaten earlier. Okay, it was a few handfuls. I like to imagine
that certain foods are lighter in the calorie count column when you can
see through them. But my tight pants wouldn't allow me to live in my
little dream world. I couldn't breathe there.

Now I was way over my allowance for the day and I was quite sad. If I wanted to see results at the scale by the end of the week, I would have to cut back over the next few days. Very sad, indeed.

It was such hard discipline, I contemplated putting off my dieting and weight loss goals for another week. A week when there were more invisible type foods that tasted delicious but didn't tip my food count upside down. But again, my pants reminded me to return to reality. I tried again to breathe.

I've known since my post-college weight-loss days, when I lost the poundage from semesters of late night pizza and ice cream cookie sandwiches, that I need to keep a food and fitness journal to stay on track. It just works. It keeps me accountable and. . .remembering (as I recall, memory is a precious commodity that. . .uh, where was I?).

I just wish that apple pie counted as one fruit serving, and one bread or grain. I wish spinach-artichoke dip could be marked as one dairy serving and three vegetables. (Yes, I can eat a lot of it.) I mean, imagine the possibilities of this: coconut or carrot cake, and lemon pound cake (wait, we really need to work on the name of that one!). But there is even hope for the potato chip here.

Then I wake up, once again, to reality. The reality that each year I grow older, my food intake has to decrease to maintain my weight. A friend of mine commiserates, "By the time I'm an old lady, I'll be down to a saltine cracker a day." If only my body were as forgiving as God is! Now that would be the ultimate diet. No journaling required.

SNEAKY APPETITES AND OTHER WOES

VALORIE QUESENBERRY

*One who is full loathes honey from the comb,
but to the hungry even what is bitter tastes sweet.*

PROVERBS 27:7 NIV

I had just enjoyed a scrumptious meal. My taste buds were doing the high kick; my tummy was celebrating. My brain was planning—a diet.

Yes, in the morning, I am going to start a diet. After all, it's only food. I can practice self-control. If I just keep focused on the goal, I can exercise willpower.

The blarney kept rolling through my mind. It sounded just wonderful. *Imagine. . .in just a few months I can be shopping for clothes in a new size, and I will feel so proud of myself!*

It was a great plan. Even Garfield, the chubby cat with the notorious nonchalant attitude, couldn't have felt more confident. The problem was that I was charting the course while sitting safely in the harbor and totally downplaying the troubling spots along the route.

You've been there. While suffering with exquisite agony after a Thanksgiving meal, abstinence from food seems an easy goal. As the Proverbs writer puts it, the thought of food is almost loathsome.

But, oh honey, wait a few hours. There's a little process called digestion taking place inside right now. And when the assembly line shuts down on that meal, the foreman will be calling for the next. And I know very few stomachs that can long resist that demand.

So, once again, hunger trumps the perfect plan. Unfortunately, sooner or later, the dieter must confront the ugly little foe of appetite.

One complication is that our poor stomachs have been conditioned to desire the unhealthiest things. The writer of Proverbs used honeycomb to illustrate a choice delicacy; I'm not sure I would have an appetite for that even after a fast. Now, wave a funnel cake under my nose, and in normal conditions, I'd be sorely tempted.

But one thing is the same, no matter what culture you live in—the ebb and flow of appetite is certain. The sensation of hunger comes and goes; fullness lasts only a few hours. What every dieter needs is a determination to observe proper boundaries no matter the physical feeling that is most obvious at the moment. Then, whether it's honeycomb or funnel cake being served, she can approach it with appreciation and restraint.

Come to think of it, that's not a bad way to approach life in general. As believers, our lives should not be subject to the sensation of the moment, but rather be guided by principles of moderation and balance. It makes every aspect of life a lot more palatable.

DEAD TO DOUGHNUTS

VALORIE QUESENBERRY

*Even so consider yourselves also dead to
sin and your relation to it broken.*
ROMANS 6:11 AMP

I have this thing with pastry. I believe my predilection is genetic, and the gene for it is decidedly dominant. Doughnuts transmit a frequency that I receive loud and clear.

In my town, we have a Krispy Kreme doughnut shop. They make them right there, letting you visually enter into the world of temptation. It starts with a sign outside that proclaims HOT DOUGHNUTS NOW in glowing neon letters. Once inside, you can watch through the big glass window as the little dough blobs are shaped, fried, flipped, and glazed right before your eyes. When you actually make it to the counter after standing in a serpentine line of addicts, the sales clerk walks back to the conveyor belt and packages those hot and fresh dripping rings and hands you a box of unbelievable caloric content.

Fat grams have never tasted so good! But in all honesty, the taste is so rich, even an addict can only consume a couple at a time. But that doesn't mean the relationship is severed completely; there's always a next time.

Now we all know what a doughnut indulgence does for the waistline. You can't hide it for long. The secret meetings are sweet, but the public results are not. Finally, something has to be done; the connection cannot continue. It's time for drastic measures.

While the Bible does not label eating doughnuts a sin (thank goodness!), it is specific about how to take care of a wrong relationship— consider yourself dead to it. No spark there, no exchange of interest, no possibility of giving in.

On the larger scale of life, if I am to overcome in my spiritual life, I have to live as though I am dead to sinful indulgence. It has no hold on me.

If I am to have victory in my battle for weight control, I must consider myself dead to the control of food. My relation to it must be broken.

Thankfully, unlike sin, I don't have to give up food completely. I need it to live and I can still enjoy it without going to excess. But I don't have to obey it; rather I make it obey me.

In verse 16 of this same chapter in Romans, the apostle Paul reminds us that if we obey something, we are its slave. Now, I really love doughnuts, but not that much. I refuse to be a slave to a dough ring with white glaze.

So, I have to let that relationship die. From now on, enjoying a doughnut must be on my terms. And while I may mourn the loss for a little while, this kind of death gives birth to a new life of satisfaction, self-control, and enhanced enjoyment. Because delectable as it is, it's only a doughnut, after all.

VISIONS OF SUGARPLUMS:
PERSPECTIVE

I'm not overweight.
I'm just nine inches too short.
SHELLEY WINTERS

AVOID COMPARISONS. . .
AND DESSERT

TINA KRAUSE

We do not dare to classify or compare ourselves. . . .
When they measure themselves by themselves and
compare themselves with themselves, they are not wise.
2 CORINTHIANS 10:12 NIV

My adult son Jeff and I chatted over lunch. In passing, Jeff mentioned the recent photo his pastor's family had just taken. The pastor and his wife are in their fifties, but they look forty. Both are athletic: She runs marathons and he lifts weights. What's more, they, their children, and grandchildren are magazine-cover gorgeous.

"You should see, Mom," Jeff explained. "They took the photo on the beach, wearing white shirts. . . ." Having met Jeff's pastor and his family, I could envision them perfectly posed with gleaming white smiles, a gentle breeze tousling their sun-kissed hair, and crisp white shirts accenting the sky-blue backdrop on a pristine beach.

"Even their in-laws are good looking," Jeff added between bites.

"Can you imagine if *we* had a family photo taken at the beach?" I mused.

Jeff choked with laughter. "Yeah, wind-blown hair, dead fish at our feet, the kids shaking seaweed off of their fingers, and we adults trying to suck in our guts!"

"Do their physical beauty and firm thighs hold no bounds?" I retorted while perusing the dessert menu. Attempting to rescue my deflated ego, I said with a serious, pompous air, "But you know, Jeff, the Bible says that man looks on the outward appearance, but God views the heart."

Jeff volleyed a snappy response. "I know. But the entire family is made up of really good Christians who love the Lord."

Of course I knew that, but the green-eyed monster spewed, "Well that's just plain sickening!"

Our conversation reflected what the Bible warns against. Namely, it is unwise to compare ourselves with others. Yet who among us hasn't gazed at a magazine cover photo, wishing to look as svelte and beautiful as the featured model? Or who hasn't walked into a gym—dressed in sweat pants and an oversize shirt—dreaming one day to look as toned and trimmed as the girl flaunting Spandex?

Though counterproductive, our sinful nature lures us to compare ourselves with others as we succumb to envy over another's talents, possessions, or appearance. Yet desiring what someone else has, is, or can do, leads to jealousy and jealousy leads to sin.

God teaches us to avoid comparisons. We are all unique in our individuality and the Bible encourages us to acknowledge, use, and give thanks for what we have and who we are. The outside is beautiful when it reflects the inner working of the Holy Spirit. In turn, that produces a godly contentment that is of great (spiritual, not physical!) gain (see 1 Timothy 6:6).

The apostle Paul likened Christians to the physical body, each member serving a specific purpose. He said, "a body, though one, has many parts" (1 Corinthians 12:12 NIV). Right now, however, I wish I had a few less plump "parts" to this body of mine. Maybe I should have considered that before ordering dessert.

WHERE DOES FAT GO?

ARDYTHE KOLB

*I praise You because I am fearfully and wonderfully made;
your works are wonderful, I know that full well.*

PSALM 139:14 NIV

Most people who diet have similar complaints. When we gain weight, it settles in the least attractive places—for me it's around my waist and in those "saddle bags" I carry. But when I lose, the only spots that seem smaller are my ear lobes. And maybe legs.

I've always had skinny legs. I'll never forget one time when I was pregnant and a neighbor said, "You look like a balloon balanced on two toothpicks." She's not on my list of best friends or fond memories. (Why is the word *tact* so similar to *tacky*?)

But really, I don't understand why it's so hard to arrange our pounds. There's a fitness center right across the street in our community. I work out regularly with a friend. At least twice a month she calls and asks, "You want to walk?"

"Sure. Meet you in a few minutes."

By the time I put on my sneakers, grab a bottle of water, and cross the street, I'd really rather just visit. But we persevere. I walk a mile and work with a couple of machines that are designed to make my abs tight, legs strong, and arms supple. She spends the time on a treadmill. Then we're both in the mood for a healthy snack—like cookies—but neither of us mentions it.

Does weight really matter so much? Take a tour of an art gallery and check out some of the artistic pieces by old masters—those Renaissance paintings that should be R-rated. None of the reclining figures look like Barbie. Even Mona Lisa wasn't skinny. The ladies who posed for those paintings carried more pounds than our society calls beautiful, but do you suppose the models worried about being a little fleshy? Obviously they didn't have managers that badgered them: "If you don't do South Beach or Atkins and start working out you won't get any more jobs." The artists must not have been bothered by their size either—the women were lovely and plump.

Compare them with models in today's fashion magazines. Many of them look stiff and their bones show. They never smile. Maybe they're hungry.

We weren't designed to focus on our size and shape except to stay as healthy as possible. Some people become so obsessed with food and exercise that they're very annoying to anyone who doesn't share their passion. Have you ever invited a friend to dinner and wound up listening to an endless diatribe about the evils of sugar and fat? You've served a scrumptious lasagna dinner with chocolate cake for dessert, and you know the friendship is shaky.

The Lord had more important work for us to do than merely concentrating on our looks. The Bible doesn't tell us to go tell others about the latest diet. How about sharing the good news that Jesus loves us just the way we are? We are definitely fearfully and wonderfully made.

THE M&M'S MYSTERY

JANICE HANNA

"And lead us not into temptation,
but deliver us from the evil one."
MATTHEW 6:13 NIV

Those who struggle with emotional issues can attest to the fact that our food consumption can become closely linked to how we feel. We feel great, and we celebrate with food. We get depressed, and we feed ourselves to dull the pain. Unfortunately, putting on extra pounds only causes us to be more depressed, so we find ourselves in a vicious cycle.

I found myself caught up in an emotional eating binge once while on a stressful phone conversation. The person on the other end of the line had just skated across my last nerve, so I reached for an M&M out of the bowl on the counter. Didn't think much about it at the time.

The intensity of the phone conversation carried on, and I vaguely remember reaching into the bowl a second time, and maybe a third. On and on the conversation went, getting me completely worked up.

Man, did I get upset! By the time I hung up the phone, I looked over at the bowl, horrified to find it completely empty. Somehow, without even realizing it, I'd eaten an entire bowl of candies. What? No way! And I hadn't even enjoyed one bite. Talk about feeling cheated. And guilty.

Great. Now I was dealing with both angst toward the person on the phone and guilt over what I'd done. Oh well. Nothing a cheeseburger and fries couldn't remedy, right? Off I went to make myself feel better. Only, in the end, I felt even worse.

Can you relate? Do you ever reach for food when you're upset? If so, join the crowd. Most of us pacify ourselves with yummy delights, convinced we'll feel better. Only, in the end, we usually feel stuffed—and guilty. What a vicious cycle!

Oh, the woes of emotional eating! Worst of all, we don't even have the pleasure of enjoying the food when it's going down so quickly. Why do we do it, and what can we do to stop it? We've got to stay focused. When those emotions kick in, face them head on and deal with them in a godly way.

Here are a few "pick me ups" you can try if you're struggling with emotional eating. First, take your eyes off yourself and do something for someone else today. Take an elderly neighbor for a drive or deliver a meal to a sick friend. Second, get some exercise. Exercise will often lift you out of the doldrums. Finally, be careful not to give in to the temptation to feed your sadness, particularly with sugars. God is standing by, ready to take your cares and sorrows. Give them to Him. Don't feed them. And the next time you do the wrong thing—say, consume an entire bowl of M&M's because you're upset at someone—don't give in to the guilt. It will only propel you to eat even more. Instead, turn to the One who is capable of healing all emotions. His plan of action is even more tasty, and it won't add cellulite to your thighs.

LET IT ALL HANG OUT

Charm is deceptive, and beauty is fleeting;
but a woman who fears the LORD is to be praised.
PROVERBS 31:30 NIV

They say when girls get together, they talk about the three *b*'s: boys, boobs, and babies. Hey girlfriend, let's hit all three!

A few years ago, I was blessed to lose forty pounds. But to my chagrin, that's not all I lost. My heaping C cups became scant teaspoons. Yep, after hanging around faithfully for over thirty years, my bosom buds, the Bobbing Twins—Freddie and Flopsie—were the first to evacuate.

I felt like I was going through puberty again, but in reverse. When I was a chubby twelve-year-old, the Lord bestowed on me some major knockers. I had to buy minimizing bras that squished and flattened to avoid knocking a tooth out during PE. In high school, the football players laughed at me struggling to harness my bouncing cleavage while running stadiums.

But since my weight loss, old sports bras just hang limp. During tennis matches, they actually creep out my armholes and flap behind me in the breeze. For some reason my opponents find this distracting.

Now I've been forced to explore the complex world of padded bras—cotton, gel, water, push-up. The only trouble with push-up is that you must have *something* to push up. So I've been reduced to buying bras akin to pre-molded cereal bowls lined with Kotex. Without them, I look like a giant Gumby—you can't tell whether I'm coming or going.

I do miss Freddie and Flopsie. Not just mere body appendages, they were little friends. When I was pregnant, I talked to them: "Freddie, stop bouncing or you'll knock me off this bike," or "Flopsie, you're gonna have to squeeze into this DDD cup; there is no E!"

And later when I was nursing my baby while talking on the phone and fixing dinner simultaneously, they stretched like rubber bands to assume any position necessary to do their jobs. They even wrapped themselves around pot handles when necessary.

Now really, would any other friends go to such great lengths for you?

Even my sixty-something friend Ellen, who lost over one-hundred pounds, is amazed at her bosom's versatility. Her breasts, once ripe melons, now sag to her knees like deflated blimps. But she doesn't let that get her down! She simply scoops them up and tucks them into her bra each morning, arranging and plumping them to form cleavage. She likens it to preparing her feather pillow for a good night's sleep.

The Bible reminds us that outer beauty is fleeting—here today, gone tonight. Try as we might, we can't capture and hold on to it for very long. But inner beauty, the kind that comes from a refreshing, dynamic relationship with Papa God, now *that* kind of beauty stretches into eternity.

And it doesn't even need a pot handle to prove its worth!

DRESSING THE PART

SHELLEY R. LEE

We justify our actions by appearances;
God examines our motives.
PROVERBS 21:2 MSG

She was goddess-like in perfect little black workout pants. Every head restrained from looking directly at her as she bobbed into the coffee shop, sweat beads still lingering on her forehead. Her sculpted fitness inspired me, yet an honest look inside myself revealed a halting twinge of jealousy.

Really? I silently scolded myself. *You don't know her. You don't know her struggles, her story. . .and even if you did, your jealousy is way off the path you should be on!*

*Urggggh. . .*my ugly humanness is so humbling!

It got me thinking about the reasons I have for working out and looking better, and wearing the cool workout attire that I sometimes enjoy (only when I'm feeling good about my body, which is another story entirely).

Some people are professional fitness people, their often flattering fashion a workout uniform. Their motivation contains a great deal of necessity. These are the sculpted fitness pros of the world, helping common Americans get it together in the diet and fitness departments. There are other people who find workout attire of various forms simply comfortable, so they wear it to class, or to relax in or run their errands. True fitness folk might call these people wannabes, but I think they mostly just wanna wear the comfy, trendy gear. Then there are those like the goddess, who are *actually working out*. I feel my jealousy creeping back up.

Motives. Those things that only God truly knows full well, even when we think we are hiding them. Even when we think we know ourselves.

So I questioned myself again. What are *my* motives for fitness and for wearing the cute workout wear? I emphasize *my* motives because, let's be real, examining them is a full-time job all by itself. If I'm working on myself, I have no time to scrutinize or think about someone else's motives (see Matthew 5:5).

Just as I resolved to keep myself in check, I remembered another woman in a completely different inspiring outfit. She wore a floppy, neon-green cotton sun hat and was beating me by half a lap in the first of the only two 5K competitions I've ever done (or probably ever will do). I am merely a fitness runner, in the game to keep my weight under control. So, I was running a terrible race but had entered the track where people are cheering and watching every move, as if the floppy hat lady and I were strategizing. I admit, I thought that if this lady, twenty years older than me and wearing a sun hat, beat me I would be embarrassed. So I picked up my pace to pass an upper middle-aged gimping man in a knee brace, en route to the final stretch, and I passed up the floppy green-hatted lady.

Truly, that woman inspires me today, to just get out there however I can and keep my motives in check.

THE REAL DEAL HEART SMART

SHELLEY R. LEE

Keep vigilant watch over your heart; that's where life starts.
PROVERBS 4:23 MSG

Less salt. Less caffeine. Less cholesterol. Low fat foods? Count your calories. Ugggh.

Whatever happened to the youthful days of eating whatever I wanted? I know they are long gone, but I like to reminisce about the days when I was a child.

In reality (i.e., real time, today, actual state of affairs), I do count those carbs, calories, points, and fat grams. Not all of them all of the time, for sanity's sake. But I just try to keep working at it. It makes a difference in my weight, my heart, and my overall health.

Regular cardio gets worked into the schedule. You know, the self-imposed-because-the-doctor-recommended-it stress test. "Isn't stress hard on my heart? Must I add cardio, too?" I asked the doctor who stared at me blankly.

Some people need to work on their sense of humor.

Okay, I get it. I must keep myself physically moving on a regular basis, and my heart will let me know if it is struggling. I was told that one indicator of trouble would be if I feel short of breath, and not just the out-of-shape kind (I hope I can tell the difference). Another indicator is if I get extremely fatigued by a walk or a run.

So, I work at it pretty much daily, keeping watch over my weight, my heart, and my health. I believe it's worth the effort.

Here's the problem: It doesn't matter how hard I work at it, I want to see tangible results in the mirror, and it's never good enough for me.

I can work out like crazy, eat like a rabbit, and get down a size or two smaller to buy that outfit that I'm sure would make me look amazing. But when I look in the mirror I am still not happy. I am still not good enough. I need to lose more, tone more, get a face-lift!

Okay, I know I don't need to get so drastic, but my constant dissatisfaction with myself reveals much deeper things in my heart. Now I am referring to the heart that is not as tangible, but is the control room of my life.

My heart often forgets why I am working at my diet and fitness. It gets caught up in acceptance, pride, and perceived power. I get quietly bumped ever-so-slightly off course, and before I know it, I cannot see the healthy path on which I was running (okay, sometimes crawling).

My heart needs to be reminded, exercised if you will, over and over again to keep me vigilant. In the deepest, broadest sense, my heart remains the most challenging muscle to train.

OF COMIC STRIPS AND FEASTS

VALORIE QUESENBERRY

The cheerful heart has a continual feast.
PROVERBS 15:15 NIV

Happiness and food often go together. It does in the world of Garfield, the lovable and notoriously indulgent comic-strip cat. On the other hand, diets symbolize misery if you're the character Cathy, whose struggles often mirror our own.

If God created a comic strip to symbolize His feeling about food, it might surprise you. God likes feasts. There is nothing about our God that is stingy, meager, or paltry. Just read the Old Testament: It's chockfull of commands to keep certain feast days, and joyful reminders to celebrate special occasions with food.

Jesus commemorated the Passover feast with His disciples. And someday in the New Jerusalem, those who belong to Christ will enjoy the great marriage feast He has prepared for His bride, the church.

God created and approves a sense of abundance and splendor.

He used the word *feast* in the Bible to convey the delightful emotions of plenty, celebration, and joy. The scripture says His very nature is characterized by abundance. He is lavish in love and abounding in mercy. After all, He gave the most extravagant gift ever—His Son—to pay the price of our redemption.

It's a revelation to realize that God isn't against feasting; dieters everywhere can rejoice. But He does oppose gluttony. In contrast to the happy overtones of the word *feast*, the feeling associated with gluttony is negative. It brings to mind words like *greed, gorge, binge,* and *misery.*

One of the rotten things about dieting is the feeling of restriction. But that may be because we have a wrong perception of boundaries. A sense of healthy restriction isn't something to shun, but rather to embrace.

A feast without boundaries is a gorge. An eater without boundaries is a glutton. Neither picture is very pretty, though many comic strips sure get a laugh out of it. And to be honest, those little characters and their problems with overeating are funny. We see our own struggle in their foibles. And it's true that we often put way too much emphasis on being a certain size. But there is no humor in unrestrained appetites, no matter how much we identify with Cathy's obsession with food and laugh at her diet attempts.

On the other hand, the writer of Proverbs compares inner joy with a continual feast. The truly happy person has a continual feast in many aspects of life. Her heart can be cheerful because she knows how to find true fulfillment in life. She indulges often in laughter; she is generous with encouragement; she celebrates God's daily gifts; and she approaches life with appreciation and zest, but not greed. And when she sits down at the dinner table, she can be sure her food is seasoned with the best spice of all—moderation. That attitude marks a real feast.

Tops and Bottoms

Laura Freudig

*But who are you, a human being, to talk back to God? "Shall what is
formed say to the one who formed it, 'Why did you make me like this?'"
Does not the potter have the right to make out of the same lump of clay
some pottery for special purposes and some for common use?*
Romans 9:20–21 NIV

I come from a family of vegetables. The men, with their big bellies,
barrel chests, and thin legs, look like ripe tomatoes drying on the
vine. The women are more like pears, with soft stomachs and ample
behinds. Some of us exercise, some of us diet; but mostly we wear our
shapes with a grudging acceptance, interspersed with periodic bouts of
lettuce-eating and jogging.

On a family vacation when I was a teenager, my mother was going
through one of those periods of asceticism. As we left our New England
city and crossed the Mason-Dixon Line to visit our relatives in the
South, my mother found it harder and harder to stick to her regimen

of eating lettuce and cottage cheese, and taking daily four-mile walks. We seemed to leave salads and al dente vegetables behind, and enter a country of pies, rolls, buttery okra, and green beans cooked for hours in pressure cookers. And forget about a daily walk: It was too hot to go outside, and, well, there might be *snakes*!

One night after another huge, buttery, cake-topped meal, my mom was moaning to her cousin Beth-Lee about her lack of willpower in the diet department. Beth-Lee was lively and chatty and hilarious, pear-shaped like the rest of us, though she said she went faithfully every day to her exercise club. My mom was telling her that before we left on our trip, she had joined the local chapter of a weight-loss group called TOPS and had lost ten pounds.

"But in the last five hundred miles," my mother said, laughing ruefully, "I'm sure I've put most of it back on! I won't dare to show my face at TOPS when we get back home."

"What's TOPS?" Beth-Lee asked.

"Oh, it's like Weight Watchers. Weigh-ins, motivational speakers, food plans. It stands for Take off Pounds Sensibly." My mom nibbled at an after-dinner piece of celery, the only raw vegetable besides onions and potatoes she could find in Beth-Lee's kitchen.

"Ha!" said Beth-Lee, looking down at herself. "My top's okay. It's my bottom I need help with!"

"Yeah," chimed in her husband, who had been dozing in an easy chair. "They should change the name to BOTTOMS."

My mom, ever practical: "I wonder what BOTTOMS could stand for?"

We all thought for a minute or two, mentally trying out various combinations of words. Then suddenly Beth-Lee shouted out, "Got it!"

She paused for dramatic effect. "Beat off Ten Tons of Meat Sensibly!" The room erupted into hysterical laughter.

We all have things we are dissatisfied with about ourselves, be they noses, moles, personality quirks, or spiritual weaknesses. All are things given to us by God for a reason: either to teach us discipline in our overcoming them or to teach us to trust God's will in His giving them to us. I will never be a banana; so, instead, I must thank my Creator and strive to be the healthiest, most beautiful pear I can be.

MAINTAINING THE FEED LIMIT: PERSEVERANCE

Blessed are those that hunger and thirst,
for they are sticking to their diets.
UNKNOWN

THE QUEEN OF EXCUSES

JANICE HANNA

*For our struggle is not against flesh and blood, but against the rulers,
against the authorities, against the powers of this dark world
and against the spiritual forces of evil in the heavenly realms.*

EPHESIANS 6:12 NIV

From the time I was a little girl, I was pretty good at giving excuses. If you encouraged me to do something difficult—something I didn't particularly care to do—I always had a ready answer for why I couldn't possibly do it. The same held true when it came to weight issues, which I've struggled with from my late teens on. Who had the time to watch what she ate? Not me! Just ask me, and I'd tell you why. (And trust me, I could probably win you over with my elaborate story!) The result of my years of avoidance and distraction? I blossomed into a roly-poly adult, who still struggles to make the right choices.

Oh, if only I could take off a pound for every excuse I've given for not eating right. I'd be so tiny, you could carry me around in your wallet. Instead of having a go-get-it attitude about weight loss, I've become a champion at excusing myself. "I can't diet because _____." Fill in the blank with anything you like. I've probably said it.

Here are a few of my favorites. Maybe you've used them, too:

"I've dieted before, but always seem to gain it back. I just can't stand the idea that it might happen again."

"Fat people are jolly. I like being jolly."

"Being large runs in my family. We're big boned. If I lose weight, people will think I'm adopted."

"God loves me just the way I am."

"I have to eat what everyone in the house eats. I can't afford to buy separate food for myself."

"Diet is *die* with a *t*."

"Fat people don't wrinkle. Who need wrinkles?"

On and on the list goes. I've gotten pretty skilled at offering a quick answer whenever someone brings up the subject of weight loss. Why? To avoid the real problem, of course. As long as I dance around it, I won't have to deal with it.

We often grow so accustomed to our list of excuses that we don't remember the Lord can deliver us from them. In fact, He longs to do just that. And He's got a plan in mind for how to accomplish it. Toss those excuses out of the window and face reality. Stop skirting the issue and look it in the eye.

Instead of excusing our poor behaviors, we need to confront them. If you're struggling with willpower issues, give them to the Lord. If you come from a family that doesn't care about weight gain, then acknowledge that and learn from it. Don't give in to the excuses without a fight.

Let down your defenses today and see what the Lord can do if you swap your I-couldn't-possibly attitude for a let's-get-with-the-program one instead. And remember, you're not wrestling against flesh and blood. It's not really your cellulite-ridden thighs or blubbery bottom that you're fighting. This is a spiritual battle. So, grab your sword and shield and prepare yourself for war!

C'mon! Get with it! No excuses.

HUMOR THY FATHER AND MOTHER

DEBORA M. COTY

Do not despise your mother when she is old.
PROVERBS 23:22 NKJV

My mother has chided me about my weight since I was a chubby eight-year-old stealing my skinny sister's cookie. Maybe it's because I was a moose in a family of munchkins. Mama's father was of slight build, five feet nothing in height, yet taller than his four daughters and granddaughters. They were all tiny, toothpick people.

Except me.

One of my childhood memories was overhearing my parents' muted conversation behind me on a walk to the park: "When Debbie walks, it looks like two dogs fighting under a blanket." I didn't know what it meant at the time, but the words embedded themselves in my mind.

As a twelve-year-old, I hit a gargantuan five feet three inches and dwarfed my teensy older cousins and aunts at family reunions. I could look down on the hair parts of most of my kin and squash them like ants if I tripped over one. To tip the scales at one hundred pounds was unheard of for our family females, and I vividly recall my mother's gasp when I scored 106 on the doctor's scales in the sixth grade.

I loved honey sandwiches and a thick coating of sugar on my cheese toast. I hid Halloween candy in my shoes and discovered that boring popcorn surpassed incredible when saturated with a whole stick of melted butter.

So Mama became the voice of my food conscience. She commented on every bite that entered my mouth until I finally left for college and indulged my newfound freedom by surpassing the freshman fifteen by ten whopping pounds.

We all have one in our lives, don't we? That well-meaning person who feels that he or she must point out—for our own good, of course—those bad habits we *should* address.

For the next thirty years, on every visit home, my petite mother never missed an opportunity to sneak in an editorial comment like, "Oh sweetheart, someone gave me these pants and I thought maybe you could wear them because they're w-a-y too big for me," or, "Better let your sister get in the backseat; I don't think you'll fit."

I knew my derriere was a sacrificial altar to the Snickers bar, but I just couldn't make a diet work. I felt frustrated like the apostle Paul in Romans 7:15: "What I don't understand about myself is that I decide one way, but then I act another, doing things I absolutely despise" (MSG). The weight insipidly escalated a few pounds every year.

Then, miracle of miracles, at age fifty I finally bit the bullet instead of Godiva. For my self-proclaimed Debbie-Do-Over year, I got invisible braces to corral my unicorn tooth, highlighted the gray, and joined Weight Watchers. By the grace of God, I shed forty pounds.

I could hardly wait for my holiday visit to my parents' home.

When Mama saw me, her jaw dropped. "Oh, my! You look terrible—all shriveled up! Here—eat a cookie!"

Sometimes you just can't win.

Faith to Do the Good Stuff

Shelley R. Lee

Let us not become weary in doing good, for at the proper
time we will reap a harvest if we do not give up.
Galatians 6:9 NIV

It was too early in January to have only logged a mile in my fitness journal. I felt so defeated as the holiday pounds stood their ground on my hips. When my time set aside for exercise rolled around, all I wanted to do was yawn and roll back over in bed.

After too many days of pathetic exercise time and lethargy (i.e., getting in the workout clothes, stretching, sighing, and finding something else to do), I pushed myself to get outside in the cold to go for a short run. After only fifteen minutes I could feel those endorphins swirling in me. Suddenly it was beautiful to be out with the light snowfall crunching under my sneakers and landing on my lashes. Really beautiful.

It was incredibly cold heading into the wind and I didn't go as far as I would have liked to, fearing I'd be numb and too far from home. So, I turned around where I knew I could clock a little over a mile in that journal sitting at home on my counter.

When I returned home, the dog and puppy wanted to play outside in the snow. I was already out there, so why not play a little? I walked with them in the yard and settled onto the snowy hammock. (I can never bear to take down the hammock for winter, so I keep it up and, wearing a warm coat, I enjoy it occasionally.)

I noticed from the hammock view that our two apple trees are angled from the prevailing west wind, and that an incredible amount of big brown seed pods were beautifully mixed in with the fresh, fluffy snow near the fence line. I would not have noticed these things from my kitchen window where I have done a lot of sighing.

The exuberant puppy rushed up to me, his sweet, snowy face pressed in toward my nose. I picked him up and rocked with him for the three beats he would permit, and he sprinted off to get a stick he had his eye on.

Somehow, after my little exercise and time outside, the sky behind the puppy and the snowflakes seemed bluer. I can't tell you for sure if it was, but I can say with certainty that I was glad I had the faith to pull myself out of my cloud of lethargy and do something good for myself. I'm never sorry when I do.

TURKEY CHILI FOR DINNER

MELANIE STILES

Children are a gift from the LORD;
they are a reward from him.
PSALM 127:3 NLT

My daughter and I made a trip to the grocery store with list in hand. Passing up the potato chips, the candy aisle, and baked goodies, we stuck to the agreement we made to eat only what was beneficial to our bodies.

My daughter is a full-time student who also works part-time. I work full-time along with writing, speaking, and teaching. We often take turns preparing or picking up dinner. Since my schedule was really packed for a full week, she was taking on the dinner challenge.

Monday morning we both prepared our breakfasts and lunches and headed out the door.

"What's for dinner?" I asked as we stepped outside.

"Turkey chili," she answered with a smile.

I backed out of the driveway, thinking our new commitment had great promise.

Dinner was piping hot and ready to be served up when I got home.

On Tuesday morning I sang the same song as I climbed into my Jeep. "What's for dinner?"

"Leftover turkey chili," she said. "We only have to cook every other night."

"That's true," I agreed, thinking fast food might be a lot easier to avoid than I had previously thought.

Tuesday evening the turkey chili was filling.

Wednesday morning I got off to a late start. I barely got my lunch together and barely made it to work on time. My daughter left a half hour before, so there was no occasion to talk about our evening meal. I had an evening writers group to teach, so it was late as I stuck my key in the lock. The aroma that met me was familiar.

"What's for dinner?" I asked, although I thought I already knew.

"I left a bowl for you in the microwave, Mom," my daughter said with a smile. I hesitated momentarily. And then I debated on whether or not to point out the obvious while my freshly made turkey chili was heating. Did my child think the only dish we could eat was turkey chili? It was late. I was tired. I decided to broach the subject later.

Thursday evening was a late night for both of us. As we staggered in, each regarded their leftover turkey chili as manna and went to bed.

Friday morning, as usual, we were heading out the door, but this time we had a minute to plan our evening.

"I'll cook today," I said. "I'll be home first. Thanks for getting us through the week. Sweetie, can I ask you a question?"

"Sure," she said.

"Why did you make only turkey chili all week? Are you thinking that is the only dish we can have for dinner?"

"No, Mom. At least I hope not. Turkey chili is the only thing I know how to cook."

In that moment I realized that my daughter was truly committed. She made good her part of our bargain, even to the point of cooking the only healthy dish in her repertoire over and over.

COMPETITION

MEREDITH LEBLANC

Let us run with endurance the race that is set before us,
fixing our eyes on Jesus.
HEBREWS 12:1–2 NASB

I plopped down in my recliner and unbuttoned my jeans. "Whew! I ate too much."

"Yeah, I've gained weight. I had to go up a size when I bought new jeans last week," my husband Jerry said.

"Yikes! We have a doctor's appointment in two months. This is not good. The last time we were in, Dr. Allen gave us an ultimatum to exercise thirty minutes each day and cut back on fatty foods. Look, bud, this is it. It is diet city big-time from here on out. No more new clothes in a bigger size, no more pizza, no more fried chicken, no more fatty foods. Are you ready to commit?"

"Looks like I don't have a choice. Are you going to give up your nightly scoop of ice cream?"

"It's only one-quarter cup." I noticed his raised eyebrow. "Okay, maybe more. Yes, I'll give it up."

"How about we have a diet competition? That'll be fun and keep us on track. Maybe a little incentive for the biggest loser."

"No way! Everyone knows men lose weight faster than women. You have the advantage."

"I'll base our weight loss on percentages to keep it fair. Now what will be the prize? I think what will incentivize me is season tickets for the Predators. You know how revved up I get for ice hockey."

"You want me to go with you?"

Jerry used his best imitation of the three Stooges, "Certainly, certainly."

"All right, if I win, you buy season tickets to the Nashville Symphony."

"Surely you don't expect me to go with you?"

"Certainly, certainly," I fired back at him. "And who is Shirley?" We both chuckled at our corny jokes.

"What kind of diet will we use? What about my old standby, the cabbage diet?"

"Let me remind you of our visit with the nutritionist just last year. I think I have the material in my files. I'll dig it out and we'll start tomorrow."

The diet was going without a snag when one Monday night we were all set to watch a football game. I made a plateful of crudités to snack on while we cheered the Titans. When a commercial for pizza came on, both of us groaned.

"Have you ever noticed they never have commercials featuring celery and carrots? I don't know why pizza once a week would hurt," Jerry said.

"Because you can't eat just one slice," I said.

The day of our appointment, Dr. Allen expressed surprise at our weight loss. "Why are you surprised? Your orders were for us to exercise and lose weight."

"Most patients don't do what I tell them."

We laughed with him and didn't share our close call of doing nothing at all. What happened with our competition? We agreed we would forgo our season tickets in favor of contributing to the Nashville Rescue Mission. We both finished, having run the race with success.

Mommy Mavens

Meredith LeBlanc

God is our refuge and strength, a very present help in trouble.
PSALM 46:1 NASB

Before the advent of online social networking, my socializing came in the form of coffee klatches with neighbors. Red Stone Arsenal employees populated my Huntsville, Alabama, neighborhood. Young stay-at-home moms with their passels of children naturally grouped together. We took turns hosting playdates for conversation on a more adult level than we would experience at home alone with our toddlers.

In the course of conversation we confessed our exasperation at not being able to lose the postpartum pounds packed into our pants. The mommy mavens could overcome teething, potty training, and thumb sucking; we would conquer those ten to twenty pounds that clung to our bellies. No longer would we raid hubby's closet for baggy shirts. No longer would we worry about seams splitting at inappropriate moments. We banded together making a covenant to nag and cheer one another on until the scale submitted to our efforts.

Each of us had unique talents to share. Terri, a fiery Italian and splendid cook, provided recipes with reduced fat and calories. Having a dinner plan is an added bonus for busy moms. Kathy, a boisterous New Yorker and avid fan of exercise, got us out with strollers in front, for a good brisk walk. She was our drill sergeant. Dot, a tall blond, shared her frugal German heritage. She loved telling us that on her family's pig farm they used everything but the squeal. Shirley, the comedian of our group, kept us laughing through trials and triumphs. Her favorite saying when dieting became difficult was "Shake it out with a good laugh. Laughter is the best medicine."

My natural role is to teach. I scoured the library for articles and books to arm us with motivation and facts. I know them all. "Nothing tastes as good as thin feels." "What you eat in private shows in public." "A diet is the penalty we pay for exceeding the feed limit." And Socrates' "Eat to live, not live to eat." We were a formidable group of determined mommies.

Dieters have certain triggers that send them running to their favorite comfort food. When the assault of depression or boredom hit, the mommy mavens were never far away. We waylaid the urge to indulge in chocolate, ice cream, potato chips, and all those guilty pleasures that soothe only temporarily. A cup of tea and a good talk worked the cure. Some days, we needed to hit the walking trail. The cure for temptation was activity and taking pleasure in success when we learned to live wisely.

Dot was the first to reach her goal weight, with Kathy not far behind. Terri celebrated her weight-loss victory next. Shirley and I had the most weight to lose, but we were not discouraged. We had a major goal to achieve. Perseverance would bring the reward of success.

The support of our group boosted our motivation and willpower. However, we realized the One who supported us without fail was our God. When we feel weak, He is strong. His wisdom is greater than this world offers. His joy brings a lasting reward.

MY FIRST TIME

MEREDITH LEBLANC

Tribulation brings about perseverance; and perseverance, proven character; and proven character, hope; and hope does not disappoint, because the love of God has been poured out within our hearts.

ROMANS 5:3–5 NASB

I've been up, I've been down, I've been lucky enough to find my higher ground. In all my days, I've hoped and prayed." These lyrics from "I've Been Down" express my dieting experience over the years. The first time I dieted, I was up.

Mother came into my room, the newspaper *Nashville Banner* in hand. "Meredith, look what I found, an article by Josephine Lowman. She's writing a column with a fourteen-day diet plan. Would you like to try it with me?"

I had never been on a diet before. Suddenly I was very aware of the bulge around my middle. *At the end of school, I did get some humiliating jabs about looking like a dumpling. Do I want my mother acting as my diet partner?*

Mom sat on the bed and rubbed my back in a comforting way. "I would like you to try it with me. We can encourage each other. You can help me prepare our food." *She must be taking courses in psychology.* I was beginning to warm to this idea. *Won't the girls be surprised when I come to school in September, looking willowy?*

"I guess that means no more chocolate pie. Do you think I need to diet?"

"Ms. Lowman says that to lose excess weight we need to cut back on how much we eat. She also suggests that we exercise as well. We'll look and feel better. I'll make some new clothes for you."

"Mom, I hate to exercise. . . . How much weight will we lose?"

"I think we will have fun if we do it together. We can put some music on and work out a routine. Ms. Lowman says we can expect to lose four to six pounds each fourteen-day period during which we follow the plan."

"What kind of clothes? Can you make a pencil skirt for me? May I buy some sweater sets?"

"Let's talk about patterns and sweaters after we reach our goal. We will probably want to follow the diet for longer than fourteen days. I think it would be good if we could each lose fifteen pounds."

The three other members of our family did not have to follow a diet. The food mom prepared for them became a huge temptation to me. I would tiptoe into the kitchen at night, hoping to sneak a bite of some delicious treat. But Mother's ears are sensitive.

"Meredith Ann, what are you doing?"

"Nothing, Mom." I couldn't get away with a thing.

We didn't have *Sweatin' to the Oldies*, but we did have old 45 records. Every morning during the week, we did our routine.

The week before school we weighed for the first time. I could tell I had lost weight because everything was loose. Mom and I yelped with excitement. I had lost fourteen pounds, only one pound shy of my goal. The bond my mother and I formed turned out to be the best part of my first experience in dieting.

Dieting Is Mourning

Valorie Quesenberry

*It is better to go to the house of mourning
than to go to the house of feasting.*
ECCLESIASTES 7:2 AMP

I'm not sure if Solomon was ever on a diet, but he sure provided a graphic visual for those of us who have. "It's better to mourn than to feast" (author's paraphrase). Yeah, if you want to be fit, that seems to be the pathway—mourning.

- Mourning because real butter has so many glorious fat grams.
- Mourning because fake cheese tastes like hydrated rubber.
- Mourning because rice cakes can never masquerade as bread.
- Mourning because the pleasure of eating is overshadowed with the irritation of measurements.

Mourning.

I guess the familiar phrase is true: "If it tastes good, it's not good for you." On the other hand, if the flavor reminds you of Styrofoam packing peanuts, you can probably consume large quantities of health food daily.

The aggravating thing is my pantry seems to know when I've started a new diet. Items that ordinarily sit calmly waiting for a future meal seem to leer at me from the shelf, begging to be discovered. Even billboards get into the act, laughing at me as I drive past their shocking displays of monstrous burgers and voluminous fountain drinks. Yes, when I contemplate the pathway to fitness, I must conclude that mourning clearly marks the way. And I confess my journey has been severely afflicted with a deep sense of reluctance. The road seems way too rough.

But ole Solomon had something to say about that, too: "Better is the end of a thing than the beginning of it, and the patient in spirit is better than the proud in spirit" (Ecclesiastes 7:8 AMP).

Okay, new thought. Sure the road is rough and the culinary scenery not that inviting, but don't forget where the pathway leads. No one chooses a diet because she enjoys saying no to food she likes; rather, she does it because the goal is extremely palatable. The promise of a healthy weight and a sense of well-being can make even Styrofoam peanuts seem appetizing. The beginning may be lousy, but the end is oh, so wonderful.

And the wise man even told us how to accomplish this prodigious task—be patient and not proud. *Patience* is believing that today matters, that every eating opportunity counts on the journey to well-being. *Patience* is knowing that there will be a day of reward. *Patience* is recognizing that there *can* be instant success in my weight loss story—I can say no immediately when I'm tempted to overeat. And that is true instant success where it really counts.

When you look at it like that, I guess I can accept mourning for a while, knowing that the goal has a taste beyond good.

Run Your Race!

Michelle Medlock Adams

*Therefore, since we are surrounded by such a great cloud of witnesses,
let us throw off everything that hinders and the sin that so easily
entangles. And let us run with perseverance the race marked out for us,
fixing our eyes on Jesus, the pioneer and perfecter of faith.*

Hebrews 12:1–2 NIV

My husband and I decided to get fit together, which sounded like a great plan. We vowed to eat healthier and jog/walk three miles, four days a week. We encouraged each other, pushed each other, and celebrated our victories. As we charted our success, I soon realized that Jeff could simply think, *I would really like to lose five pounds this week,* and *poof!* He was down another five pounds. I, on the other hand, struggled to lose every pound. As happy as I was for my precious husband to achieve his fitness goals, I would become aggravated when he lost more weight than I did every single week. I wanted to sneakily change our bathroom scale's settings so he wouldn't lose more than me just one week, you know? Sure, we joked about it, but I had to really stay focused on my goals and stop playing the comparison game or I'd work myself into a tizzy. Ever been in a tizzy?

The comparison game is really more of a trap than a game, because in a game you have a winner. There are no winners when you play the comparison game. Whether you're comparing your weight-loss progress with your spouse's weight-loss journey or the size of your backside to your best friend's derrière—it's dangerous! Growing up, whenever I'd start playing the comparison game, my mom would always say, "What is that to thee? Follow thou me" (John 21:22 KJV). Of course, that would make me mad because I knew she was right.

Jesus doesn't want us to focus on someone else's victories or even his or her defeats. He doesn't want us to measure ourselves against someone else and feel like we always come up short. No, Jesus wants us to keep our eyes on the prize, follow Him, and allow Him to transform us for the better. If we waste all of our energies worrying about someone else's accomplishments and wondering if we measure up, we'll become too distracted to experience our own victories. That's why God tells us in His Word to run our own race. He knew we would be miserable trying to run somebody else's race.

So, no matter where you are in your weight-loss journey, celebrate your accomplishments along the way. Stay clear of the comparison trap and come to the place where you can be sincerely happy for your best friend when she slips on a pair of size 4 jeans and you're still struggling to fasten your size 10s. Your goal should be to become a better you, not better than somebody else. Once we truly are free from the comparison trap, life will become so much more joyful. So, bring on the joy and kick out comparison. Your finish line is in sight—just keep pressing on!

PEANUT BUTTER DREAMS

RAMONA RICHARDS

Even youths grow tired and weary, and young men stumble and fall;
but those who hope in the LORD will renew their strength.
They will soar on wings like eagles; they will run and
not grow weary, they will walk and not be faint.

ISAIAH 40:30–31 NIV

I am a lifelong dieter. I went on my first diet just after I turned eleven. Working with my mom, I ate a diet based on the then American Dietetic Association guidelines. I don't remember much about the diet, except for what I carried for lunch every day: a sandwich made with "diet" bread and one slice of ham, eight crackers with peanut butter, an apple, and artificially sweetened tea.

That may sound meager, but compared to the cafeteria food, I had a feast. I had to guard the peanut butter and crackers carefully. To this day, peanut butter is a keystone in any diet I pursue.

I carried my lunch in an old-fashioned tin lunch box, which

was painted to look like luggage covered with stickers from foreign countries. That lunch box held my dreams—of being thin, of being a sophisticated world traveler. This was the late 60s, pre-Internet, pre-color television, even, but I had read about the world in my books. I wanted to visit Los Angeles, Madrid, London, Sydney, and Tokyo!

It was also pre-low-cost airfares. After a year, I lost enough weight that I thought I was ready. I looked good! All I needed was the right clothes, and off I'd fly. I even called an airline one rainy Saturday afternoon and asked for the price of a round-trip ticket to Los Angeles and Sydney.

My meager sixty-five dollar savings didn't quite measure up. The difference was so great that I had to laugh. My mother hugged me and told me not to worry, since all dreams start small. She told me to keep praying for God's will in my life, and everything would fall into place. We sat the lunch box on the shelf next to my piggy bank and my calorie counter. I added other dreams—easier to achieve—to the shelf, and started praying and working for them, one by one.

The weight came off and stayed away several years. Although it would be thirty years before I made it to Los Angeles, I started traveling when I was nineteen. Washington, DC, was the first stop, and one year I put twelve thousand miles on my car in just three months.

They say the best weight loss happens slowly. So do some dreams. But that's okay. We can't always see God's plan for us the first time we get down on our knees. But He'll lift us up on those eagle's wings and we'll get there. . .with a good tail wind, constant prayer, and a lot of peanut butter.

THE *I LOVE LUCY* DIET

JANICE HANNA

Therefore, since we are surrounded by such a great cloud of witnesses,
let us throw off everything that hinders and the sin that so easily
entangles. And let us run with perseverance the race marked out for us.
HEBREWS 12:1 NIV

I'm known for my zeal. My friends and family members would agree. I'm one of those hyper, bouncing-off-the-wall, always-ready-to-get-going sort of girls. And never has the zealot in me been more at home than during a good diet. If you've ever lost a few pounds, you probably know what I mean.

I went on my first crash diet at the tender age of fifteen. I'd gotten up to a shocking (gasp!) 130 pounds. If you'd asked me then, I would've said I was the fattest girl on the planet. If you'd ask me now, I'd say, "One hundred and thirty? What I wouldn't give to weigh 130 again!" It's all a matter of perspective, isn't it!

Back then I had an added incentive to lose the weight. My dad, hoping to entice me to do the right thing, decided to up the ante, offering me a new car for my sixteenth birthday if I dropped from 130 to 105, my target weight. Talk about a motivation! I spent the next several weeks on a crash diet that rivaled the now-famous *I Love Lucy* episode where she nearly starved herself to death trying to lose enough weight to be in a show at the Tropicana. I jumped in headfirst and dieted, dieted, dieted. In many ways, I took to the task like a lion tamer, ready to conquer the wild beast within.

I conquered the beast, all right. For a while, anyway. And somewhere along the way I discovered that I had a dieting zealot living inside of me. Likely she'd always been there, she just couldn't find her way out through the layers. I dropped the first ten or twenty pounds and the world began to take notice. As soon as people started asking the questions, I started giving the answers. I thought I had them all, since the weight was coming off so easily. Six weeks after starting my diet, I'd dropped down to 105. Voila!

It lasted about three days. Then, over a period of months—*after* I had the keys to that new car in hand—the weight came back on. All of it, and more.

Can you relate? Ever been there? Sometimes we bite off more than we can chew (pun intended), especially when it comes to controlling our weight. We decide to take off a few pounds. We're convinced we can do it quickly and effectively and rapidly jump into the latest plan of action. Unfortunately, we often try to do too much too quickly. We want to lose a lot of weight. Fast. We want to fit into a new swimsuit in a couple of weeks. We want to impress an old friend we haven't seen in years. It takes a while to figure out that getting into shape takes time. If we set small, attainable goals, we will be more likely to achieve them. Setting large, unrealistic goals is a surefire setup for failure.

These days, I'm not so quick to crash diet. I've learned my lesson. Slow and steady is the way to go. I'm pretty sure even Lucy would agree!

Not So Deep Sleep

Ramona Richards

Trust in the Lord with all your heart, and lean
not on your own understanding; in all your ways
acknowledge Him, and He shall direct your paths.

Proverbs 3:5–6 nkjv

Of all the odd ways I've tried to lose weight, group hypnotism has to be one of the most unusual. I'd heard that it worked with individuals, so when a hypnotist offered to work with a group of women at my church, I was curious.

At the first session, about twenty-five women showed up. We paid our fee, then had coffee and snacks, while we socialized with the hypnotist. Brad—young, handsome, and charismatic—charmed us all, making us feel more comfortable in his presence. Then we all sat and he explained, in a deliciously melodious voice, what would happen next. He'd teach us techniques for self-hypnosis, and once we were under, he'd offer guidance and suggestions for the weight loss.

In the week between the sessions, we'd keep a journal, meet once to discuss our progress, then come back next week for more instructions. To me it sounded like group therapy with a twist, but I tried to keep an open mind.

So we sat, eyes closed, as he counted and we breathed. Five deep breaths, in and out slowly. . .one. . .two. . .*I wonder why Janice cut her hair so short. She knows she doesn't look—stop it! Breathe! Four. . .five. . . then shallow breaths and count down from 100 backward. One hundred. . . ninety-nine. . .ninety-eight. . .Brad's really cute. He'd make a good model for the hero of my next book. Although he'd need to be a little more—stop it! Where was I? Eighty-nine. . .eighty-eight. . .no, eighty-three. . .eighty-two. . .*

Apparently, I'm not a good candidate for hypnosis. A friend who went with me suggested I might be a better candidate for ADD medication. To be fair, a number of women did lose weight while going to Brad's sessions. I mostly lost two hours a week.

But I'm glad I sat through the sessions, even if I could not relax long enough to stop analyzing what he was doing. While other women were feeling calm and open to suggestion, I was taking notes for a future novel or short story. Hypnosis was simply not my path to weight loss.

The rest of life is like that as well. My path is not your path, or her path, or his—whether in weight loss, college, career, love, family, or faith. I can't walk your path and you can't walk mine. Christ met the woman at the well while Paul had to meet Him in a blinding light on the Damascus road.

So when this diet or that isn't working, keep looking. The right path is waiting.

CRAVING HO-HO'S:
HUMOR

I've been on a constant diet for the last two decades.
I've lost a total of 789 pounds. By all accounts,
I should be hanging from a charm bracelet.
ERMA BOMBECK

LAUGH YOUR WAY TO HEALTH

JANICE HANNA

A cheerful heart is good medicine,
but a crushed spirit dries up the bones.
PROVERBS 17:22 NIV

From the time I was a little girl, I was the happy-go-lucky sort. Giggly. Goofy. A laugh a minute. My mom always called me a ham because of my overly dramatic style. Now that I think about it, comparing me to a pig was probably where my weight struggles began. Not that I minded the insinuation that people found me entertaining. Oh no. Anything I could do to get attention was all right with me. As long as it was the right kind of attention. And making people laugh was the icing on my proverbial slice of chocolate cake.

Then I grew up. . .and life happened. Unfortunately, some of the events of my grown-up life weren't funny. In fact, they were pretty tragic. Some wondered how I pulled through, let alone maintained my sense of humor. Still, through my faith and my innate desire to keep on keepin' on, I managed to keep my smile intact much of the time. The joy of the Lord gave me a strength I'd never known.

So, what does this have to do with weight loss? Everything! The Bible says that laughter is good for us. It's like a medicine, in fact— one that actually tastes good and has no side effects! It's God's way of softening the blows of life. And I can think of no greater salve for the chubby soul than a great sense of humor. It's truly a gift from on high. Besides, if you don't laugh, you're bound to cry. Weight struggles can really get you down if you let them. At times they seem wholly unfair. I mean, c'mon. . . . Your friend eats a cheeseburger, fries, and milkshake and stays trim. You eat a banana and gain three pounds. Who can explain it?

There's really only one way we can possibly maneuver the tricky road from tubby to trim—we've got to maintain our God-given sense of humor, even when the going gets tough. Otherwise every bump in the road will be an excuse to do the wrong thing.

Besides, laughter is good for you! Did you realize it strengthens the immune system and burns calories? It's true! It's also great exercise for the diaphragm and the abdominal wall muscles. And laughter releases endorphins, too, so we feel better after a belly laugh. (Ha! Get it? *Belly* laugh?) See? Doesn't chuckling make you feel better? There's no better way to lighten the load than through laughter. Best of all, it's contagious, spreading to those around you faster than the common cold, and binding you together in a way that no other emotion can.

Instead of focusing on how unfair your weight struggles might be, make up your mind to giggle your way through them. And trust God. He's got big plans for you, no pun intended. He wants to use you in mighty ways and needs you to be in good shape to accomplish that. So, hang on for the ride as you set out to eat right and get healthy. You can triumph in Him, one laugh at a time! It's simply a matter of mind over platter.

SPITTING PRIDE

SHELLEY R. LEE

A man's pride will bring him low,
but a humble spirit will obtain honor.
PROVERBS 29:23 NASB

Should I ever get prideful in my diet and fitness journey, not to worry; God is ever watchful over me. I smile as I count some of His ways.

More than one time on the roadside, I have not wanted people in an oncoming car to see me walking, so I would start running when I saw a car and would walk again when the driver and his or her passengers were far enough away not to see me. Pathetic, I know.

One time I was running by a group of guys and feeling rather powerful (I should mention here that I have a great imagination). Unfortunately, I didn't see that pothole along the side of the road, so I rolled my ankle and nearly ate gravel covered in tears. I was so embarrassed that, with watery eyes and a very sore ankle, I just kept attempting to run through the awful stumble as if nothing had happened.

One of my favorite episodes, now that I'm way past it, is when I could not figure out for the life of me how to use a particular exercise machine. I did the best I could with it while musclemen worked out on machines nearby. Later, when I saw them use the machine properly, I realized I'd been sitting on it backward and working a completely different muscle group. I felt. . .absolutely *brilliant*. Wow, I can be an idiot at times.

Another embarrassing occasion involved my spitting, an activity that needs to occur every now and then when I'm working out. One time, while running along the country roads, I made an effort to improve my skills in this department. Unfortunately, I miscalculated the wind resistance, and my projections were way off. Shall I say, it got a little dicey and embarrassing when witnessed by passersby?

Another day the wind was blowing so hard that I felt as if I were running in place like a cartoon character; then, when I merely opened my mouth, spit blew out wildly onto my face. This was a laugh God let me have with just Him and me. I appreciate it when He does that. Because I get it, I really do.

I need to be reminded of my fallen state and subsequent need for His grace. It helps me extend that same grace to those around me. Thanks, God!

CURE FOR THE COMMON. . .GRAVITY

LAURA FREUDIG

A merry heart maketh a cheerful countenance: but by sorrow
of the heart the spirit is broken. . . . All the days of the afflicted are evil:
but he that is of a merry heart hath a continual feast.
PROVERBS 15:13, 15 KJV

It was a Rube Goldberg kind of accident.

Have you ever seen drawings of this inventor's fantastic contraptions, complex and multistepped, that accomplish nothing more than cracking an egg or turning on a light bulb? Mechanical arms swing up and down, balls roll down inclines, pulleys whirr, levers shift weights which drop into buckets, which tip and pour water on to waterwheels, which spin handles, which release hamsters, which run on treadmills. . .you get the idea. A small amount of actual work is accomplished with a tremendous amount of extraneous effort.

Her accident followed the same progression.

She was trying to do a video step-aerobic workout in her living room, all part of her New Year's resolution to shape up, slim down, and start treating her body more like the temple of the. . .well, if not the Holy Spirit, at least a bit *less* like the temple of the Twinkies and the Cheetos. In the middle of a tricky, foot-tangling step-behind-and-slide-to-the-side move called the grapevine, she decided to turn up the volume on the TV. That, in a manner of speaking, released the hamster.

She leaned forward to reach the remote, but the top of her foot caught on her step, tipping her sideways. She tried to steady herself against the bookcase, but her hand knocked against a lamp sitting on top, which began to topple. She reached for the lamp with one hand, the edge of the bookcase with the other, but missed them both because her feet were entangled with each other and the now tipped-up step. It hit her in the shin; she fell forward into the TV, which tipped over, landing on her leg. The cordless phone and the remote, which had both been on top of the TV, skittered and spun to a stop by her left hand.

Twenty minutes later she found herself staring up at fluorescent lights and ceiling tiles as two paramedics wheeled her into the emergency room. Her leg throbbed in rhythm with her heartbeat. A doctor leaned over her, his stethoscope dangling a few inches above her nose. He asked about her accident, and then said, "Are you allergic to anything?"

She looked up. "Gravity."

Suddenly the mood in the hallway changed. The gurney swerved slightly as the two paramedics let out loud guffaws. The doctor's serious face cracked into a wide grin. Oddly, the throbbing in her leg faded slightly.

"Well, I guess we don't have to x-ray your sense of humor," he said.

Her leg did turn out to be broken, a greenstick fracture of the femur that left her in the hospital for days, in pain for weeks, and in a cast for months. But her merry heart never left her, and she could truly say when the cast came off that, despite weeks of sponge baths, callused armpits from crutches, and a perpetual itch behind her knee that she couldn't scratch, God had given her a continual feast. Levity is the best cure for gravity.

Step Lightly

Ramona Richards

*Then our mouth was filled with laughter, and our tongue
with singing. Then they said among the nations,
"The LORD has done great things for them."*

Psalm 126:2 NKJV

I once heard a Christian motivational speaker say that learning to laugh at yourself was the first step to maturity. If that's true, I started to mature early.

I've been clumsy all my life. My mother says it's because I'm left-handed; my brother says it's because I talk too much and don't pay attention where I'm going. I do have a tendency to list slightly to the right when I walk, and I frequently trip over my own feet and run into walls.

As a kid, I wanted to be lithe and elegant, and have people say, "Ooh" when I walked by, not, "Watch out!" and "Are you okay?" I wanted to have the sleek beauty of a wild palomino, not the properties of the average tumbleweed.

But God had other plans for me. I may be a klutz, but He gave me a sense of humor and a quick wit. A gift for words, a heart for people, and a love of teaching. He showed me how to use my sense of humor to reach people, and to turn my clumsy adventures into wonderful stories.

Also, He gave me really good friends with a similar outlook. When I was in high school, two of my best friends—both more than six feet tall, blond, and rail thin—would go with me to the mall. I'd walk between them, with my short, round, redheaded looks, and we'd count the double takes. When I'd trip over my own feet, I'd tell folks that I was falling over cracks not yet there. And when my klutziness turned a wilderness hike into a hair-raising adventure, I wrote it up and sold it to a boy's magazine—one of my first professional sales.

I developed the same humor about my weight and dieting, as well— not because I wanted to be the "jolly fat girl" or laugh at myself before anyone else did, but because there's something inherently humorous about the human condition and the hoops we make ourselves leap through. We strive to be thin, even knowing God loves us as we are. I want people to be able to love themselves—and laugh at themselves— when the time is right.

God has given us the gift of humor to help us out when our lives are tumultuous, as well as when they are smooth and easygoing. Laughter helps rebuild hope because it reminds us of the good times in our past and that we'll be able to have those again. It helps us carry on and find hope, whether we've experienced a personal loss—or a significant weight gain.

It even helped me have less interest in being thin than in being the woman God meant me to be—even when I'm tumbling down a hill.

FUDGING FIGURES:
BALANCE

A balanced diet is a cookie in each hand.
UNKNOWN

It's the Little Things

 Ardythe Kolb

Catch for us the foxes, the little foxes that ruin the vineyards.
Song of Solomon 2:15 NIV

As a secretary, one of the "other duties as assigned" in my job description was to keep a well-stocked candy dish. Naturally, I didn't want to offer something without making sure it was safe, so I tasted it regularly. Just one piece at a time.

Every diet-conscious person understands that little bites don't matter in the big picture, so it hardly pays to count Skittles, peppermints, or malt balls. Figuring calories is confusing because the manufacturer's idea of a "serving size" is much more than one or two pieces. The math gets tedious. Why bother?

When I bake, I can't stand to waste any batter that's left in the bowl. It's such a tiny amount. Then after the cake or pie or other confection is done and we've eaten part of it, I'm sure that just a forkful—every time I walk through the kitchen—won't make any difference.

My grandmother was overweight, but it was easy to see why. She took huge servings at meals, especially desserts, and when candy was offered, she filled both hands. I don't do that—I'm very careful about what I eat.

But one day as I tussled with my jeans, I said to my husband, "Gee, I can hardly get these on!"

"Maybe you should lose a few pounds."

Of all the nerve! "You see what I eat—I barely have anything on my plate. My metabolism must be out of whack or something—maybe it's hormones." I finally got the jeans over my hips and jerked at the zipper.

"What about that bag of M&M's you bought yesterday? Or the Jelly Bellys in the pantry?"

He was getting on my nerves. "What do you mean? I only eat one or two pieces. Who are you to talk? You grab a handful."

"Yeah, but I'm not worried about how my clothes fit! Besides, you may just take a few at a time, but think about how often you hit the candy bowl. You know, a little bit, a lot of times, equals a whole bunch!" He turned around and wandered off. I heard him snicker.

How could he be so inconsiderate? Snatching some baggy sweats from the shelf, I hopped around as I struggled and wiggled to rid myself of those offensive jeans. But one foot got caught in the leg, and I tumbled to the floor. I scrambled to right myself before he came to investigate the racket. A couple jelly beans helped assuage my injured pride.

I finally got around to actually noticing how many little bites I consumed every day. *Maybe I do need to cut back. The nutritional value I lose probably won't cause scurvy or any other dreadful disease—it might even be healthier.* I hated to admit it, but my husband was right. All those small pieces could be like the little foxes that ruin the vines. They definitely added up and eventually caused trouble.

CHOCOLATE MAKES MY JEANS SHRINK

DEBORA M. COTY

It is good and fitting for one to eat and drink,
and to enjoy the good of all his labor.
ECCLESIASTES 5:18 NKJV

Did you know that the average American consumes 11.7 pounds of chocolate each year? That's roughly the weight of a lawn chair! Why, if not for chocolate, there would be little need for stretch denim. Or control panels. Or female subterfuge.

I mean, really, which of us hasn't stashed Tootsie Rolls amongst the potted plants? Or hidden M&M's in her ibuprofen bottle? Or buried telltale Snickers wrappers inside balled-up paper towels in the trash can?

A friend with a secret choco-addiction once confided that her bamboozled husband, after taking out the garbage, couldn't fathom why there were empty chocolate icing cans at the bottom of every trash can in the house. He couldn't remember eating even one cake!

Of course, there are the health issues of chocolate consumption to consider. I certainly don't plan to condemn myself to an early grave because I selfishly refuse to sacrificially down my daily Dove bar. Why, look at Peggy Griffith of Abbotsham, UK. This feisty one-hundred-year-old claims she's eaten 30 chocolate bars per week (that's approximately four *each day*) for over 90 years, which translates to over 14,000 pounds of chocolate.

This granny's got game!

Now if you think about it statistically, it makes zero sense to say no-no to cocoa when you consider that a chocolate bar contains about 500 calories. At just one per day, that's 3,500 calories per week, which roughly equals one pound of body weight—an intake of 156 pounds over a three-year period. For the average 140-pound woman, that means that without chocolate, she would have disappeared six months ago.

See. . .our very lives depend upon chocolate!

Even researchers at Johns Hopkins University attest to the medical benefits of chocolate. They found that flavanol in dark chocolate thins the blood and helps prevent heart attack and stroke just like aspirin. One small caveat, however: To match the effects of a daily baby aspirin, the dosage would have to be two chocolate bars. That's 1,000 extra calories *each day*.

Hmm. A food exchange could even it out. For health's sake, I would be willing to sacrifice green and yellow foods to accommodate the extra brown food intake. It's not my fault they happen to be vegetables.

We *can* indulge in that delightful, creamy, delicious stuff, but we must strike a balance. A balance in our nutrition, our diets, and our greed.

This theory was reinforced as I recently checked out of the grocery store. The elderly woman in front of me, purchasing a jug of milk and a loaf of bread, sized up my stack of Lean Cuisines, topped with three gigantic Cadbury bars. Her wrinkled face suddenly lit up with a coy grin. As she reached for a Hershey's bar on the candy rack, she confided with a knowing wink, "Life's all about *balance,* isn't it, dear?"

WEEPING WENDY

MEREDITH LEBLANC

*Keep your conscience clear. For some people
have deliberately violated their consciences.*
1 TIMOTHY 1:19 NLT

Women try everything conceivable to lose weight—wiring their jaws shut, hypnosis, and every fad diet that comes down the pike, as well as diet centers. For five years I owned a weight-loss franchise. I could tell stories aplenty of deception, failure, and successes as folks came to me for help. This is one of those stories.

"I have been on a million diets, and I never have had any luck," Wendy said.

I could see the tears welling in her eyes. "Every success starts with one step. Are you ready for that first step?"

That first month Wendy dropped pounds quickly. She came in each visit with her food journal filled in. "I love behavioral guidance and coming to the center."

Then the second month she hovered in a yo-yo pattern—down a pound, up two. "I told you diets don't work for me. This one isn't any different."

"Come back to my office. Let's go over your meals." I noticed her entries for fruit did not specify what kind and how much. "Wendy, why haven't you listed the kind of fruit you eat and how much?"

"Is that important? I follow the food plan."

"Let's go back and see if you can recall what you ate and the amount, starting three weeks ago."

She squirmed in her seat, and her eyes filled with tears. "I went to the farmer's market a few weeks ago and bought a bushel of nectarines. My husband and kids ate about half of them, and I have eaten the rest," she said.

"Do you remember the serving is only one-half of a fruit for two meals each day?" I handed her a box of tissues.

"Yeah, but if I don't eat them, they will go bad."

"How many nectarines are you eating each day?"

More squirming. "Four or five. It's fruit after all. How bad can fruit be for you?"

"I think we both know the answer to that." I pulled out the *Eat Smart Guide* and flipped to the *N* section. "Look at this, Wendy. There are 88 calories in one medium nectarine. If you eat five a day, that totals 440 calories, 352 calories more than you need for each day. Do you think that's why you aren't losing weight?"

She burst into tears. "I knew I shouldn't have eaten that many. They are so good."

"What did your husband say when he found out?"

"Oh, he doesn't know. I went back to the market and bought some more."

"Are you eating those, too?"

"Well, yes. I told you, I can't let them go to waste."

"Wendy, don't deceive yourself. Stick with the right portions."

Wendy reached her goal weight. Her testimony is, "I can laugh about it now. At the time, I thought I could deceive everyone, but the scale told the story. I celebrate two successes today, my goal weight and learning that honesty pays."

BORROWING POINTS

MICHELLE MEDLOCK ADAMS

*For I say, through the grace given unto me, to every man that is among you,
not to think of himself more highly than he ought to think; but to think
soberly, according as God hath dealt to every man the measure of faith.*

ROMANS 12:3 KJV

I've pretty much tried every diet program known to man or woman.
Usually, I get talked into starting a new diet plan by a relative who
doesn't want to go the diet journey alone. That's exactly what happened
last year when my niece called and asked me to go to a weight-loss
meeting with her. Wanting to drop a few pounds that I'd gained over
the holidays, I agreed and met her at the church where weigh-ins were
already underway when I arrived. After stripping down to the bare
minimum (the most I could take off without being arrested) and being
weighed in, we sat down in the next room to learn the particulars of
this very popular diet program.

I discovered the amount of points I could eat in one day and how many floater points I had available for the entire week. Next, we discussed high-point meals versus low-point options. I took notes and realized quickly how much I despised this program. First, I would have to restrict my eating to practically nothing, and I'd have to do math—two of my least favorite things. Nevertheless, I embarked on this point-driven plan the following morning. But by day four, I desperately desired my favorite sugary cereal for breakfast, so I allowed myself to have it. After devouring every single Fruity Pebble, I did the math. Yikes! I had consumed fifteen points of my daily allotted nineteen points in one meal! By two that afternoon, I was totally out of points and there were many hours remaining before bedtime. By 8 p.m., I was very hungry and began complaining to my husband, Jeff, about my lack of points. He smiled his Grinchy smile and teased, "You can borrow some of my points." Real funny, eh? If I'd had enough strength, I would've throttled him but I was too weak with hunger to react. I went to bed hungry that night and vowed to use my points more wisely in the future.

Unfortunately, we can't borrow eating plan points or spiritual points from our spouses or anyone else for that matter. It would be so much easier to rely on Jeff for everything—including extra eating plan points when I've used all of mine—but it just doesn't work that way. As much as he loves me, Jeff can't hear from God for me. He can't read the Bible for me. He can't do the things for me that I need to do to grow in the Lord anymore than he can give me his eating plan points and expect me to lose weight. At some point, we have to grow up and take responsibility for our own lives, doing what we know to do even when it's uncomfortable, inconvenient, or difficult. We can respect our loved ones and their faith, but we can't borrow it. So, do the dos and grow up spiritually! Oh, and while you're at it, enjoy three Jolly Ranchers. They'll only cost you one point!

Butter Is Good for the Soul

Jo Russell

What good will it be for someone to gain the whole world,
yet forfeit their soul? Or what can anyone give in exchange for their soul?
Matthew 16:26 NIV

Ginny and I met for breakfast at a down-home restaurant halfway between our two towns. It was our girls' day out. The café is so popular that unless you bring a tow truck to make a parking place in the crowded dirt lot behind the building, you're walking there from a block away.

Inside the little café was a warm smell of fresh coffee and bacon. While Ginny and I settled ourselves at our table, I noted the red-checked curtains and pine walls. It felt as welcoming as a farm kitchen.

While we perused the menu, we noticed servers rushing with platters to get hot food to the customers. Ginny, a health teacher, wrinkled her nose at the food fare: eggs doing the breaststroke in butter, home fries dripping with enough oil to keep McDonald's going for a month, buttered toast and a pile of jams teetering on the edge of a plate.

The menu was not a problem for me. I decided what healthy items I could choose from the menu: two-egg veggie omelet, hash browns, and water with a slice of lemon.

Ginny is committed to health and hates fat more than germs. She decided she would have to modify this order *a great deal!*

When the waitress approached us, the teacher was primed for battle. Although in her fifties, Ginny maintains a slim willowy figure. She is well-proportioned. You can think of her as a string bean.

First, the waitress took my easy order, and then, with a smile, turned to Ginny. Also well-proportioned, this middle-aged server was the perfect cucumber.

"What will you have, Miss?" asked Waitress Cucumber.

"I'll have a one-egg veggie omelet with no cheese," announced Ginny String Bean.

"Are you sure? What's an omelet without cheese?" Miss Cucumber mused.

"No cheese," my friend emphasized. "What kind of toast do you have?

"White or wheat."

"Is that a 100 percent wheat or a multigrain?"

"Just plain wheat."

"I'll have one-half slice of toast with no butter."

"No butter, miss?" repeated Waitress Cucumber. She wasn't ready to give up. "This is the real thing. Butter is good for the soul!"

"No butter!" Ginny insisted. She figured she won that round, but later I noticed she left most of her small piece of toast on her plate. No wonder. It didn't have much taste.

When we're dieting or maintaining a healthy weight, we have to reflect that we are body *and* soul. Body and soul go together like every part of an egg: shell, yolk, and white. Remember that butter is one of God's good gifts, and He's happy to let you enjoy it in moderation. Even if you are a cucumber instead of a string bean, you are God's perfect creation!

TAKE IT OFF!

MELANIE STILES

How foolish can you be? After starting your Christian lives in the Spirit,
why are you now trying to become perfect by your own human effort?
GALATIANS 3:3 NLT

Our entire building was invited to join a weight-loss group. I had just spent the morning looking in the mirror, repeating, "If I could lose the weight without a support system it would already be gone!" I immediately added my name to the list.

I showed up for my first meeting, secretly hoping, like most do, that I wouldn't be the heaviest person in the room. I also hoped the group environment would feel somewhat friendly and safe. Needless to say, my insecurities raged. The group leader welcomed me with a genuine smile as she asked me to step on the scales for my first weigh-in. It was at this moment, of course, I felt most vulnerable. Those three numbers would now be recorded in black ink on her file card. No more of my fudging or denial, at least where she was concerned. Throughout the entire process she maintained her end of our idle chitchat and to my relief, she made no shocking comments about my less than fit physique. I had survived the worst of it.

I then joined several women sitting around a conference table—our gathering place for the next eleven weeks. We tentatively performed introductions all around. A few minutes later everyone knew who worked where, and the meeting got underway. As our leader comically explained the dos and don'ts involved in the program, a kindly lady sitting next to me leaned over and whispered into my ear. "You did your weigh-in all wrong, but it's really a blessing."

"Excuse me?" I whispered back.

"Next time, take off your shoes," she replied, "and you'll automatically be down a half a pound."

The following weeks became incremental lessons in taking it off as we attempted our instant half-pound tactics. By week three, everyone was removing their shoes like it was the most natural thing in the world to do. Jackets soon hit the pile with the shoes. Yet, in every crowd there are always those who move to the absolute edge of any concept. Suddenly the weight of the fabrics we were wearing became our focus. Friday is traditionally designated "casual day" in many offices. Since we met on Fridays, many of us normally attended in blue jeans. But not after it was determined by mutual consent that denim was by far one of the heaviest materials one could wear. I became a shoe-shucking, jacket-ditching, polyester pants wearer along with the rest of them. After all, every quarter pound counted right? I particularly applied my newly learned skills if I had strayed a bit too far from the program during the week.

We lost a few pounds together, but not as much as those who didn't join in our removal system. We realized the error of our ways when there was simply nothing left to take off. God had given us the support of each other to actually take off the weight, not just our clothes. It was time to honor His gift.

WORKING OFF THE TOOTSIE ROLLS: EXERCISE

I'm in shape. Round is a shape. . .isn't it?
UNKNOWN

POWER PARTNERS

MICHELLE MEDLOCK ADAMS

"For where two or three gather in my name, there am I with them."
MATTHEW 18:20 NIV

When I first started working out, it wasn't something I longed to do. I never understood those exercise enthusiasts who said, "I love to run." I would always respond, "I love to *have* run." In other words, I like to have it over with. But I noticed a shift in my thinking as I continued on my get-fit journey. If I skipped a day or two at the gym, I missed it. That surprised me about myself. I couldn't believe that exercise had become a vital part of my life—not just an obligation.

Looking back, I crossed over because I had finally become consistent with my exercise routine long enough to experience its many benefits—sleeping better at night, fitting into my favorite jeans, feeling stronger, etc. Always before, I would start down an exercise path, do well for a few weeks, and after that, take a hiatus. Then I would start the vicious cycle all over again. What made the difference this time? I had a workout partner/drill sergeant, my youngest daughter Allyson, to keep me on track. If I said, "I'm too tired today," she would say, "Too bad. You'll feel better once you hit the treadmill." If I said, "I'll drop you at the gym and pick you up later," she'd say, "Mom, get your workout clothes on and get in the car." She wouldn't take no for an answer. So I went and I went on a regular basis for six months. After that, I was hooked. This same scenario has played out in my spiritual life, too. I used to pray a few minutes during my morning devotional time and again at the end the day. And, if something happened in between, I'd send up a few short prayers to God. But I hadn't ever committed to that concentrated, take-the-phone-off-the-hook prayer time. Then I met a woman named Susan who asked me to be her prayer partner. We committed to pray for each other every day. We'd share prayer requests and report the praise reports to one another as the miracles manifested in each of our lives. Even if I was too tired to pray, I couldn't close my eyes and say, "I'll pray extra long tomorrow," because I had made that commitment to someone else. She was relying on me, and I wasn't about to let her down. My prayer partner forced me to take my prayer life to another level.

Today, my original prayer partner is no longer my daily prayer warrior, although I still pray for her, but that pattern of committed prayer time stuck with me. Like exercise, I had experienced prayer's many benefits and longed to speak with the Father. I will forever be thankful to Susan for helping me discover the power and importance of a set prayer time. If you need a prayer partner or even a workout partner, God will send you one. Just ask Him. Or, I could send you Allyson.

WOMAN DOES NOT
LIVE BY BIKE ALONE

JO RUSSELL

*And my God will meet all your needs according
to the riches of his glory in Christ Jesus.*
PHILIPPIANS 4:19 NIV

The exercise habit had taken hold of my life even though I was over fifty. While the rest of the family members rented cars when we flew in for my son's wedding, I rented a bicycle. Having been a single mom, I reasoned that besides being healthy, a bike is cheap.

Up to the day after the wedding, my getting around the small island was easy. The rides were short and invigorating. Then I spotted a stunning plant at the hairdresser's, and I was driven to capture its beauty by finding one at a local nursery. As a plant addict, I forgot the airlines would not be enthusiastic about a four-inch pot in my carry-on.

"The nursery is just down the road a piece," the hairdresser told me. She described the route, an easy ride. It felt good getting the exercise.

"We're sold out," the salesperson told me, hose in hand, spraying down the blooming flowers. "You can try the nursery department of the home improvement store."

"Where is that?" I asked.

He said, of course, "Down the road a piece on your way out of town."

Everyone's description of "down the road a piece" was from a driver's perspective.

I pedaled until I turned up on a road surrounded by forest. No improvement store, but I kept pedaling, driven by sheer determination.

By the time I reached the store, I was seeing spots in front of my eyes. I drank most of my water and wobbled into the nursery on unsteady legs.

"We'll have more by Tuesday," the clerk cheerfully announced.

I would fly out the day before.

"How far back into town?" I asked, swaying with fatigue. I shouldn't have asked.

"Down the road a piece."

"Could you translate that into distance?"

"Oh, maybe three-and-a-half or four miles. Not far."

I unzipped my backpack. No food and little water. I needed something like an energy bar. I would have settled for a cookie, an olive, a tomato, anything! All nourishment was back at the hotel.

Heading toward town, I cranked the pedals. The slight upgrade was like a runaway truck ramp. Soon earthworms were sprinting by me. I prayed and pedaled. I stopped and drank the rest of my water.

Mosquitoes lunched on my bare arms.

Panting and dizzy, I stopped again. A dusty green van pulled over in front of me and parked. I was staring at the pavement when I heard a voice. "Hi, Mom!" my son greeted me. "Do you want a ride?" I looked up to see his smiling face poking out the window of a rental car. The whole vanload of family had been sightseeing.

I was stunned. Was it an accident they were here? No, it was God's answer to prayer. It was not an energy bar or an olive, but a ride in a green van.

God took care of a foolish senior who had gone the extra mile when she shouldn't have.

Stature of Limitations

Janet Rockey

Which of you by taking thought can add one cubit unto his stature?
Matthew 6:27 kjv

iar! I directed my accusation toward the scale in my doctor's office. That number couldn't be right. I kicked off my shoes and set my purse on a nearby chair. Did I truly believe those wardrobe items weighed thirty pounds? The scale moved a negligible space to the left.

Grumble.

The nurse led me to the exam room. She set the open folder upon the table next to my chair and took my blood pressure and pulse.

I couldn't pull my focus from the neon-sign entry under *Patient's Weight* on my chart. I presumed my metabolism had taken a nap and wondered how to wake it up. I manage an early morning walk every day, but it's more of a stroll than a stride. Spending eight hours a day in front of a computer and flopping in a recliner at night doesn't burn calories like jogging in the park or riding a bike. I have the best intentions. But when I get home from work, I'm too tired.

The nurse left, instructing me to undress and don the latest in paper gown fashions.

The doctor entered. I expected no sympathy for my weight gain from this slender, beautiful woman with a stethoscope.

"Your lab work is good," she said, scanning my chart, "except your elevated sugar levels." She looked up at me. "Cut back on your carbs and increase your leafy vegetables."

"I've already cut potatoes from my diet, replacing them with brown rice." I beamed with pride in my sacrifice.

"Brown rice, whole-wheat pasta, and whole-grain breads are better for you," Dr. Beautiful said, "but they're still carbs."

"Should I go back to potatoes?" Ever the optimist.

"Gourds like squash are better." She glanced at my chart again. "You could afford to lose a few pounds."

"I'd like to drop about thirty," I said, hoping she'd say that number was too drastic.

"Thirty would be good."

Gulp.

"What aerobic exercises do you do?" she continued.

"I walk every morning."

"Every little bit helps." She finished the physical exam and closed my file. "You can dress now. Keep walking and remember—curb the carbs."

I went home and took inventory of our pantry. Macaroni, spaghetti, and brown rice mingled with canned goods on the shelves. Note to self: *Buy squash.*

"I'm really not overweight," I argued with myself. "I'm under-tall."

I'd be at my ideal weight if my height measured six feet. Maybe I should pray for the Lord to make me taller. That would be easier than shedding unwanted pounds.

Since I can't grow in height physically, I can endeavor to grow spiritually to the measure of the stature of the fullness of Christ. Through that endeavor, I might take better care of the body He has given me—and in the process drop the excess weight.

CAN'T HIDE CELLULITE

TINA KRAUSE

He [God] will bring to light what is hidden in
darkness and will expose the motives of the heart.
1 CORINTHIANS 4:5 NIV

Each spring, more than hyacinths and daffodils burst from winter's darkness. Pale legs, shaded from the summer sun, become combustible at the first balmy rise in temperature. Some pop out, others plop, but out they come just the same.

For the ploppers among us, it is spring's first struggle—a time when we refuse to wear shorts as a matter of dignity. Colorless legs are bad enough, but ones that resemble stuffed sausages are enough to cause some of us to pray for an arctic blast in June.

So in late spring, I join those who laboriously catch the rays to tan their shapeless lard-laden legs. A bronze tone compensates for the lack of firm, been-sweating-in-the-gym-all-winter thighs, I reason. But experience reminds me that bumpy cellulite comes in all colors. You can tan it, tone it, slip pantyhose over it to hold it together, but short of liposuction or cosmetic surgery, it's a lost cause.

Yet I'm old enough to remember those antiquated machines at the gym, ones with rollers that were supposed to smooth out cellulite's lumps and bumps. The contraption was as effective as the other exercise machine of extinction that was designed to banish inches from the hips via a vibrating canvas belt. I, like many others, tried them all, and *voila!* The cellulite still dimpled under the summer sun and in winter's darkness, whenever and wherever.

Our quest to tone our legs and camouflage physical flaws is ageless. Women apply makeup and creams to contour their face, conceal wrinkles, and firm droopy eyelids tauter than a soldier's army bulk. Oversize shirts hide bulging midsections and baggy jeans lose heavy hips in a sea of denim.

Eventually, however, the camouflage is removed. The makeup is washed off at the end of the day, and unshed pounds make their seasonal debut in the summer sun.

They say, "You can run but you can't hide." But I try anyway, even with more "weighty" matters than physical flaws. I often try to conceal poor attitudes and bad habits with spiritual clichés and Sunday smiles, but sooner or later the summer sunshine of God's Word exposes my spiritual lumps, bumps, wiggles, and jiggles.

But there is hope: When our flaws meet God's Son-shine, Christ promises to forgive, heal, firm, and reshape our lives so that we'll never have to hide again.

Wish I could say the same thing about my lumpy thighs. Nevertheless, I'm off to the gym to walk a few miles and try out more contemporary exercise machines. But first I'll head to the tanning bed to apply some camouflaging. In the meantime, I am covering my cellulite with sweatpants.

These Are a Few
of My Favorite Ads

Janet Rockey

*"Why do you spend money for what is not bread,
and your wages for what does not satisfy?"*
Isaiah 55:2 nasb

While watching the continuous stream of commercials for exercise equipment and weight loss plans, a tune from *The Sound of Music* floated through my head. I apologize in advance to Julie Andrews.

*Midriff and belly and waistline reductions,
Super amphetamines and fast liposuctions,
Hawking the latest in exercise fads,
These are a few of my favorite ads.*

213

Face-lifts and butt tucks and Botox injections,
Walking on treadmills or stair-climber actions,
Specialty diets that promise you'll lose.
By eating their meals with the flavor of ooze.
"Buy our diet!
Buy our workout!
And a change you'll see!"
Believing their promise to help me begin
And soon I can say, "I'm thin!"

Yes, I have shelled out hard-earned money for exercise equipment with the hope that it would sculpt my body to match the beautiful model in the ad. After twenty faithful sessions with my new Abs Flattener, my body still didn't resemble hers. If the device worked its magic on her, why did it fail me? I'm now convinced she was born with that shape.

The instructions show how to stow the piece when not in use by easily folding it twice and sliding it under the bed or sofa. An exasperated struggle led me to finally disassemble the apparatus, putting the nuts and bolts into a Ziploc storage bag. I burned more calories taking it apart than I did using it.

A year later, while storing my Christmas tree in the guest room, I bumped something under the bed.

"What's this?" I recognized the forgotten Abs Flattener with light blue rubber handlebars. The dusty coating made me sneeze. *Sigh.* Another donation to the thrift store.

I've seen these gadgets, tapes, and books—many in like-new condition—at garage sales with evidence the seller experienced the same satisfaction I did. As I get older and, hopefully, wiser, my goal for a healthier existence doesn't include the latest fad diet or exercise equipment. I prefer to munch on a celery stick while taking a brisk walk through the park and give my hard-earned money to a ministry for the Lord.

He alone will satisfy.

Contributors

Michelle Medlock Adams is an award-winning writer, earning top honors from the Associated Press, the Society of Professional Journalists, and the Hoosier State Press Association. Author of forty-four books, Michelle has also written thousands of articles for newspapers, websites, and magazines since graduating with a journalism degree from Indiana University.

Debora M. Coty, a resident of central Florida, is an events speaker, columnist, and author of over one hundred articles and twelve books including *Too Blessed to Be Stressed: Inspiration for Climbing out of Life's Stress-Pool; More Beauty, Less Beast: Transforming Your Inner Ogre; Mom NEEDS Chocolate;* and *365 Chick-isms: Witty Musings on Life, Love, and Laughter.*

Laura Freudig has lived most of her life in the islands along the Maine coast. She enjoys reading, hiking, and singing with her husband and four children.

Janice Hanna Thompson is the author of over sixty books for the Christian market. She lives in the Houston area near her children and grandchildren. Her days are spent writing, teaching, and planting kisses on some of the sweetest cheeks in town.

Ardythe Kolb and her husband owned and operated a successful Christian bookstore for thirteen years. She now works as a full-time freelance writer and serves on the board of the Heart of America Christian Writers' Network. She loves spending time with family and friends, and enjoys travel, reading, and target practice.

Tina Krause is a freelance writer, newspaper columnist, and author of *Laughter Therapy* and Barbour gift books: *Grand Moments for Grandmothers* and *Life Is Sweet*. Her work has appeared in forty-eight magazines and nineteen book compilations. Tina and her husband, Jim, live in Valparaiso, Indiana, where they enjoy spoiling their five grandchildren.

Meredith LeBlanc is a member of ACFW and Middle Tennessee Christian Writers. She has spent the last three years learning craft and developing skills while working on her writing. Meredith enjoys her rural home in Kingston Springs, Tennessee, along with her husband, Jerry, and rescued dogs, Nick and Buddy.

Shelley R. Lee is a freelance writer who has authored numerous articles, two books, and contributed to four others, most recently, *Heavenly Humor for the Teacher's Soul* (Barbour Publishing), and is the editorial manager for WhatAVisit.com. She grew up in Michigan and earned her bachelor's degree at Grand Valley State University where she met her husband of twenty-five years, David. They reside in rural northwest Ohio with their four teen- and college-age sons and never enough groceries. She posts humorous stories regularly at www.shelleyrlee.blogspot.com.

Valorie Quesenberry is a pastor's wife, mother, author, and fellow dieter who confesses that Krispy Kreme doughnuts make any writing project more enjoyable. In addition to contributing to the Heavenly Humor series, she is the author of *Reflecting Beauty* and *Redeeming Romance* from Wesleyan Publishing House.

Ramona Richards is a writer and editor living in Tennessee. Formerly the editor of *Ideals* magazine, Ramona has also edited children's books, fiction, nonfiction, study Bibles, and reference books for major Christian publishers. She is the author of *A Moment with God for Single Parents*.

Janet Rockey is a freelance writer living in Tampa, Florida, with her husband and two cats. Her writing dedication survives a full-time job, constant home improvements, and her furry feline "children," all useful distractions to inspire her stories and novels. She serves as vice president in Word Weavers–CWG, Tampa Chapter.

Freelancer **Jo Russell** keeps laughing at everyday challenges. She experienced many while raising her sons to adulthood as a single mom. Jo has won numerous writing awards for humor. Her inspirational stories, humor, and publicity have been featured in northeast Arizona newspapers and dozens of magazines including *Arizona Highways*.

Melanie Stiles has accumulated hundreds of bylines in various publications. She uses her background to share joys, hardships, and other life journeys with her fellow man (or woman). Her favorite life experience to date is when her eight-year-old granddaughter rushes through the front door of her home, yelling, "Yaya! I'm here!"

Scripture Index

OTHER HEAVENLY HUMOR TITLES
FROM BARBOUR PUBLISHING

Heavenly Humor for the
Cat Lover's Soul

Heavenly Humor for the
Dog Lover's Soul

Heavenly Humor for the
Woman's Soul

Heavenly Humor for the
Chocolate Lover's Soul

Heavenly Humor for the
Mother's Soul

Heavenly Humor for the
Teacher's Soul